AWESOME
Outdoor Science Experiments
for Kids

AWESOME OUTDOOR SCIENCE EXPERIMENTS for Kids

50+ STEAM PROJECTS AND WHY THEY WORK

DR. MEGAN OLIVIA HALL, PhD, NBCT

ROCKRIDGE PRESS

For general information on our other products and services or to obtain technical support, please contact our Customer Care Department within the United States at (866) 744-2665, or outside the United States at (510) 253-0500.

Rockridge Press publishes its books in a variety of electronic and print formats. Some content that appears in print may not be available in electronic books, and vice versa.

Series Designer: Katy Brown
Interior and Cover Designer: Richard Tapp
Art Producer: Sue Bischofberger
Editor: Alyson Penn
Production Editor: Andrew Yackira
Production Manager: Jose Olivera

Illustration © 2021 Collaborate Agency. Recurring patterns used under license from iStockphoto.com. Photography used under license from shutterstock.com, cover and p. viii. Photography used under license from iStockphoto.com, pp. ii, 148, and back cover. Author photo courtesy of Rebecca Palmer.

ISBN: Print 978-1-64876-936-8 | eBook 978-1-64876-937-5

R0

For Leo Kirkaldy
Bickelhaupt, the best
outdoor adventure buddy
anyone could ever have.

CONTENTS

INTRODUCTION

Awesome Outdoor Science Experiments for Kids is a treasure trove of adventure, with over 50 fun experiments that focus on science, technology, engineering, arts, and mathematics (STEAM). As you explore the chapters of this book, you will discover the science of photosynthesis, technologies that predict weather, how to engineer shelters that will keep you warm in all kinds of weather, art forms that show off nature's beauty, the amazing math of gravity, and so much more!

This book is for readers ages 5 to 10 who love going outside and are curious about the outdoors. Have you ever wondered what makes leaves turn color in the fall, why every snowflake is different, or how to bring butterflies together? If so, this is the book for you!

I'm a science, robotics, and agriculture teacher in a public school in Saint Paul, Minnesota. My school students enjoy learning science outside, even in the snowy winter! I'm also a mom to one daughter and one son. Our family camps in the summer, gathers leaves in the autumn, cross-country skis in the winter, and hunts flowers in the spring.

Exploring the world with kids always opens my heart to a sense of wonder and keeps me connected to what matters most. Whether I'm listening to birds sing or enjoying the peaceful hush of a winter snowfall, being outside calms my heart and fills me with joy. From the smallest snail's shell to the most enormous galaxy in the night sky, nature gives us endless opportunities to explore, wonder, understand, and appreciate our world. I hope that as you do the experiments in this book, you will enjoy getting outside and being connected with the great outdoors just as much as I do.

I'm passionate about STEAM, because science, technology, engineering, arts, and mathematics each offer a different way to interact with and understand nature. I think our world is amazing, and I want to know how it all works—the waves in the ocean, the clouds in the sky, the seeds growing in the earth—all of it! Whether you're conducting a science experiment, applying a technology, engineering a solution, creating art, or calculating math, every time you use STEAM, you get to know more and more about this wonderful world.

This book is organized into chapters, with each chapter diving into one STEAM component through 10 or more outdoor experiments. An outdoor experiment is an experiment that engages kids in understanding the science behind nature through hands-on learning. Outdoor experiments use mostly natural materials found outdoors and can also be performed anywhere outdoors.

In the book, you will find over 50 fun experiments. Every experiment will include information on the time needed to complete it, the difficulty level, lists of materials, step-by-step instructions, the hows and whys behind the experiment, details about the STEAM components featured, and fun ideas for extending the experiment to learn even more. The book also has a glossary of **bolded terms** and their definitions. Just flip to the back of the book to look up any of the featured fantastic STEAM words.

Each experiment practices the scientific method, the approach that STEAM professionals take to explore and solve mysteries.

The scientific method begins when we ask a question. Next, we form a hypothesis, or an educated guess about what answers we might find. Then we do an experiment that tests the hypothesis, observing what happens. At the end, it's time to conclude: did the observations support the hypothesis? A true experiment asks and seeks to answer questions that haven't been answered yet. Otherwise, it's just a demonstration.

These experiments are meant to be performed by young scientists anywhere outdoors with minimal adult supervision. When adult help is required, there will be a "Caution" warning added to the experiment.

Special spotlights at the end of each chapter focus on a science career. Be sure to learn about the careers that relate to the outdoor experiments you've been performing—you might discover your destiny as a future outdoor scientist!

Once you understand the principles of STEAM, you will see them everywhere. Whether walking along a city sidewalk, hiking in the woods, swimming in the ocean, or flying in an airplane, you will notice the science, technology, engineering, art, and math behind everything that's happening in the real world, and that is truly AWESOME!

Chapter One

HOW TO USE THIS BOOK

Welcome to *Awesome Outdoor Science*
Experiments for Kids! In this book, over 50 experiments are organized by categories: science, technology, engineering, arts, and mathematics—Ⓢ Ⓣ Ⓔ Ⓐ Ⓜ. Many of the experiments in this book could be listed in multiple categories, because STEAM involves lots of interaction. For example, an experiment in which you build a tool to measure the speed of wind combines mechanical engineering (through building), science (because you are studying weather), and math (by measuring with numbers). Each experiment will include a box explaining the STEAM categories at work. As you explore outdoors, you'll learn so much about the science of nature by using the scientific method to observe (or notice) and hypothesize (or guess) what will happen in each experiment.

GETTING READY

To begin, choose an experiment that looks fun and interesting. There's no need to start at the beginning of the book. You can skip all around. Outdoor science includes so many topics that you are sure to find many fantastic projects. Whether you like butterflies, moss, oceans, or the moon, you will see experiments that spark your curiosity.

Once you have chosen an experiment, read the question paragraph. It will explain the goal of the experiment and pose a question. Do your best to predict an answer to the question. This prediction is your hypothesis. Your hypothesis is your best guess. Your experiment will either support or contradict your hypothesis. If your experiment contradicts your hypothesis, that's actually a good thing! Many STEAM professionals test predictions in order to disprove them. Making discoveries that disprove predictions and change ideas is an important part of the STEAM process.

For safety, be sure to check for any cautions listed in an experiment. For example, some experiments may require safety gear, like goggles, or adult supervision. STEAM experiments are the most fun when everyone is safe.

As you are choosing an experiment, check the time needed and the level of difficulty. *Easy* means that the experiment has 5 steps or fewer, usually takes less than 30 minutes, and is fairly simple for younger kids (ages 5 to 6) to complete. *Medium* means that the experiment has 10 steps or fewer, usually takes 30 minutes to an hour (or more), and is suitable for kids ages 7 to 8. *Hard* means that the experiment has more than 10 steps, can take at least an hour to perform, and is challenging for kids ages 9 to 10.

Finally, check the materials list for your experiment. Most of the experiments in this book can be completed with materials that you will find outdoors and a few everyday tools. You may want to invest in a simple magnifying glass or hand lens and an inexpensive but sturdy thermometer. Many outdoor scientists carry what is called an armored thermometer, a thermometer in a plastic holder that prevents breaking. For many of the experiments, you will need a sturdy bucket.

THE SCIENTIFIC METHOD

Awesome Outdoor Science Experiments for Kids is an interactive guide that will lead you through authentic investigations organized according to the scientific method. As STEAM professionals work, they cycle through the steps of the scientific method, sometimes revisiting or revising certain steps depending on the direction their experiments take. Each experiment in this book includes the following steps of the scientific method:

- ➲ Explore a question
- ➲ Form a hypothesis
- ➲ Test the hypothesis
- ➲ Collect and analyze data
- ➲ Draw conclusions about the hypothesis
- ➲ Consider future investigations

The scientific method is extremely helpful to scientists because it is organized, consistent, and easy to communicate, even for scientists from different cultures and countries.

You may notice that many experiments in this book involve more than one experimental setup. Each setup will have one difference from the others. Comparing the results from these different setups is a math skill that's very important in science. Pay attention to how changing just one factor, or variable, affects your data.

DOING THE EXPERIMENT

Begin each experiment by reading the question paragraph. This introductory paragraph will explain the topic and what the experiment is trying to do. As you explore the topic, there may be words that are new to you. These will be written in **bold** and are defined in the glossary at the back of the book.

Next, consider what you think will happen in the experiment and write down your hypothesis in the "Hypothesis" section. Continue preparing by looking for any cautions listed for the experiment. Consider the level of difficulty and the amount of time needed for the experiment.

Then gather the materials and remember that many of the supplies may be found outdoors.

Once you have your supplies, follow the step-by-step instructions to test your hypothesis. This is my favorite part of any experiment, and I hope you love it, too. Be sure to wait until you've tried the experiment for yourself before you read the "Hows & Whys" section that explains the science behind the investigation.

Take a moment to notice the STEAM connections in the experiments. Many experiments can fall under multiple STEAM categories. For example, creating a moss garden with buttermilk and moss spores involves both science and art.

The "Now Try This!" section shows ways to vary the experiment or take it to the next level. If you enjoy an experiment, this is a great way to extend your fun and learn even more.

Remember, even failed experiments are educational. Many of the world's greatest STEAM discoveries came from failed experiments. No matter what happens, every experiment that you attempt will deepen your learning, strengthen your STEAM skills, and help you grow into an even more fabulous scientist. Unexpected results are all part of the fun! Relax and enjoy your journey through the wild world of outdoor science.

Chapter Two

SCIENCE

Every field of science has a connection to the outdoors. **Physics**, the science of matter, energy, and the forces in the universe, includes studies of the sun, moon, stars, and planets. Chemistry, the study of matter, is everywhere outdoors—in the air, the water, and the soil. The outdoors is full of living things, and since life is the focus of biology, many biologists do their work outdoors. Earth's landforms, rocks, and minerals are all important to geologists, who explore the science of the earth.

In this chapter, you will explore the science of the outdoors by studying how trees breathe, why the moon changes, how bugs talk, and more! In each experiment, you will be following the scientific method. Taking the time to predict what will happen by writing a hypothesis is key. After you've collected data, go back to your hypothesis to decide if it was supported by your data.

BREATHING UNDERWATER

LEVEL OF DIFFICULTY: EASY

MESSY METER: MINOR MESS

FROM BEGINNING TO END:
20 MINUTES

SEASONS:

In the winter, fresh spinach leaves from the grocery store work well for this experiment. Spinach is a sun-loving plant.

MATERIALS

- ➔ 1 leaf from a plant growing in the sun. Sun-loving plants include daises, pansies and most trees.
- ➔ 1 leaf from a plant growing in the shade. Shade-loving plants include hostas, ferns, and hydrangeas.
- ➔ 2 clear cups
- ➔ Enough water to fill the cups
- ➔ Sunbeam

? Plants capture the sun's energy in a process called **photosynthesis**. During photosynthesis, leaves make oxygen. Oxygen bubbles are easy to see if you put leaves underwater. ***Will leaves from a sun-loving plant make more bubbles than leaves from a shade-loving plant?***

Hypothesis: _____

_____

THE STEPS

1. Go outdoors and gently pick the leaves from 2 different plants. One plant should be growing in the sun, and the other should be growing in the shade. Take only 1 leaf from each plant so that the plant can keep growing after your experiment.

2. Fill the cups with the water.

3. Put the leaves from the sun-loving plant in 1 cup of water and the leaves from the shade-loving plant in the other cup of water. The leaves will float.

4. Place both cups in a sunbeam and watch for bubbles to appear. Notice if one leaf makes more bubbles than the other leaf.

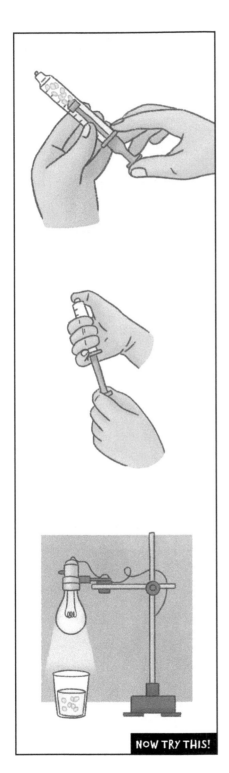

NOW TRY THIS!

HOWS & WHYS: During photosynthesis, plants use the energy in sunlight to turn water from the ground and carbon dioxide in the air into sugar and oxygen. The oxygen floats out of the leaves and into the air. Animals breathe the oxygen in, use it to break down food in their bodies, and breathe out carbon dioxide. In this experiment, the oxygen bubbles stuck to the leaf underwater—where you could see them! Plants that grow in the sun can usually photosynthesize very fast in bright light. Shade-loving plants usually photosynthesize at a slow but steady rate.

S T E A M Here you are applying plant biology and chemistry to learn how quickly photosynthesis works in the leaves of two different plants.

Now Try This!: To learn more about how leaves make oxygen bubbles during photosynthesis, try using a straw to punch small disks out of your leaves. Mix a pinch of baking soda and a few drops of dish soap in a cup of water. Fill a syringe with this mixture and add the leaf disks to the mixture in the syringe. Create a vacuum by pulling on the syringe plunger while your finger is covering the opening of the syringe. Pull the plunger completely out and then pour the leaf disks and water mixture into the cup. Place the cup in bright light. The leaf disks will sink at first because your vacuum pulled all of the air out of them, but, as they photosynthesize the oxygen bubbles will make them float.

STEAMY LEAVES

LEVEL OF DIFFICULTY: EASY
MESSY METER: MINOR MESS
FROM BEGINNING TO END:
1 HOUR
SEASONS:

In the winter, houseplants work well for this experiment. You will need two different kinds of houseplants. Try to find houseplants with tough and soft leaves.

MATERIALS

- ➔ 3 large zip-top plastic bags
- ➔ Tree
- ➔ Bush or shrub
- ➔ A short, soft plant, like a flower or grass plant

 Plants do more than photosynthesize. Plants also pull water from deep underground, moving it through their trunks and stems, and let out water vapor through their leaves. **What kind of plant lets out the most water: a tree, a shrub, or a flower?**

Hypothesis: ....

....

Caution: Never place a plastic bag near your face or head.

THE STEPS

1. On a sunny day, place a zip-top bag over the leaves at the end of the branch of a tree. Zip the bag as far closed as you can without squashing any of the leaves.

2. Repeat with a bush or a shrub.

3. Repeat with a short, soft plant, like a flower or grass plant.

4. After 20 minutes, come back and look at all 3 bags. Do you see water droplets inside? Which plant has the most droplets?

HOWS & WHYS: Leaves have small openings called **stomata** that let carbon dioxide in for photosynthesis, the process by which plants make food using energy from sunlight. Stomata also let a lot of water out of leaves. The more a plant photosynthesizes, the more water it loses through its stomata. A big maple tree can lose almost 60 gallons of water in just 1 hour! The amount of water lost doesn't just depend on the size of the plant. Plants growing in dry areas like deserts save water by making their leaves as thick and little as possible. The needles on a cactus are actually water-saving leaves! Big, soft leaves will let out more water than tough, thick, small leaves.

S T E A M The plastic bags you used in this activity are a form of technology. By comparing the amounts of water lost by each type of plant, you are also doing math.

Now Try This!: In the daytime, plants photosynthesize. All day and all night, plants also do **cellular respiration**, the process of breaking down sugars made in photosynthesis to release carbon dioxide and water. To see evidence of cellular respiration in a plant, place a dry zip-top bag around some of its leaves after the sun has gone down. All of the water you collect in the bag will be from cellular respiration.

MOON WALK

LEVEL OF DIFFICULTY:
MEDIUM
MESSY METER: MINOR MESS
FROM BEGINNING TO END:
15 MINUTES
SEASONS:

MATERIALS

- ➔ A moonlit night
- ➔ Flashlight
- ➔ Round rock or ball

 Some nights, the moon is a bright circle in the sky. Other nights, it can be a half circle or crescent. Scientists call these shapes **phases**. In this experiment, you will observe the moon in the night sky and make moon phases with a flashlight and a rock. **Why do you think the moon changes phases?**

Hypothesis: ....

....

! **Caution:** Stay close to your home when going outdoors at night.

THE STEPS

1. Go outside on a moonlit night, find the moon, and match its shape to its phase using the diagram below. Is the moon full, new, or somewhere in between?

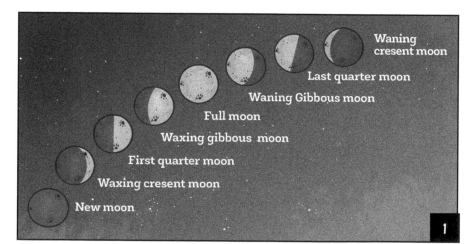

AWESOME OUTDOOR SCIENCE EXPERIMENTS FOR KIDS

2. Have a friend, sibling, or adult stand to your side and turn on the flashlight. The flashlight represents the sun.

3. Hold a round rock or ball out in front of you, between you and the flashlight. Notice that the side of the rock nearest you is dark, just like a new moon.

4. Now hold the rock behind you, so you are standing between the "moon" (the rock) and the "sun" (the flashlight). The side of the rock nearest you should be bright, just like the full moon. If your body is blocking all of the light, try holding the flashlight a little to one side of your body to let some of the light shine on the rock.

5. Move the rock in a circle around your body while the other person holds the flashlight still. Try to make the rock look like the moon appears tonight. Why does the rock look different when you hold it in different places?

CONTINUED

HOWS & WHYS: The moon **orbits**, or circles, Earth about once each month. Because of this, we have a different view of the moon every night. Light from the sun always shines on half of the moon. We see all, part, or none of the bright side of the moon depending on where the moon is in its orbit around Earth. In this experiment, you created a **model** of moon phases using a flashlight (the sun), a rock (the moon), and Earth (you).

S T E A M Astronomy is the field of science that involves studying our moon and sun, as well as all of the other moons, suns, and planets in the universe. Making models, like the one you created of the sun, moon, and Earth, is an important skill in engineering and math.

Now Try This!: Did you know that the moon rises in the east, just like the sun? The moon rises at a different time of day or night, depending on its phase. Try keeping a moon journal: Every evening before you go to bed, sketch the moon and note where it is in the sky.

ECLIPSE ON A STICK

LEVEL OF DIFFICULTY:
MEDIUM
MESSY METER: MINOR MESS
FROM BEGINNING TO END:
30 MINUTES
SEASONS:

? Every 18 months, the sun is **eclipsed**, or cast in shadow, so that it seems to disappear somewhere on Earth, and the sky becomes as dark as night. The moon can be eclipsed, too; this happens about every 6 months. In this experiment, you will build a model that will answer the question: **Why does an eclipse happen?**

Hypothesis: ....

....

MATERIALS

- 2 rubber bands
- 2 short sticks, about 5 inches (15 centimeters) in length
- 1 (3-foot) stick
- 2 ounces playdough or clay
- A sunny day, around noon

THE STEPS

1. Use a rubber band to attach one of the short sticks to one end of the long stick.

CONTINUED

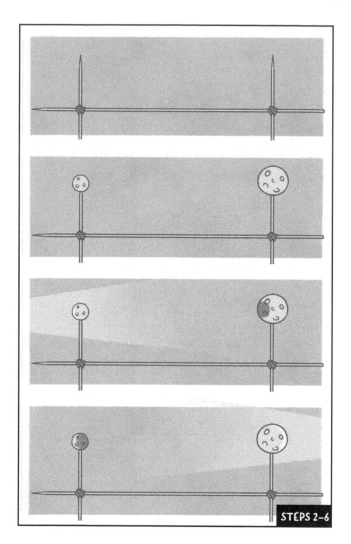

STEPS 2–6

2. With the other rubber band, attach the other short stick to the other end of the long stick.

3. Make a small ball of playdough, about ½ inch (1 centimeter) in diameter and a bigger ball, about 2 inches (5 centimeters) in diameter.

4. Push the playdough balls onto the small sticks at the ends of the big stick.

5. Hold your model under bright sunlight, with the little ball up high and the big ball down low. Try to get the shadow of the little ball to land on the big ball. This is an eclipse of the sun.

6. Flip your model and try to get the shadow of the big ball to land on the little ball. This is an eclipse of the moon. Was this easier or harder than step 5?

HOWS & WHYS: An eclipse happens when a shadow covers the sun or moon. In your model, the larger ball represented Earth and the small ball represented the moon. When a shadow from the small ball fell on the large ball, you modeled an eclipse of the sun. When the shadow from the large ball landed on the small ball, you modeled an eclipse of the moon. The sun, Earth, and moon have to line up just right for an eclipse to happen, which is why an eclipse is a special event.

S T E A M When you built the model, you were applying mechanical engineering skills. When you noticed that it was easier to eclipse the moon than the sun in step 5, you were using math by comparing the sizes of the shadows of the Earth and moon.

Now Try This!: Are you interested in seeing an eclipse for yourself? Do an Internet search using the term "eclipse calendar" and you will see a list of upcoming solar (sun) and **lunar** (moon) eclipses. If you can't be in the location of an eclipse, you will be able to find video streaming of the eclipse that you can watch from home.

PHENOLOGY BINGO

LEVEL OF DIFFICULTY:
MEDIUM

MESSY METER: MINOR MESS

FROM BEGINNING TO END:
1 HOUR

SEASONS:

MATERIALS

- Card stock
- Pencil
- Comfortable outdoor clothing and shoes
- Hand lens or magnifying glass (optional)
- Binoculars (optional)

 Phenology is the study of how living things experience the seasons. Plants and animals respond to nature's changes in many ways. In this experiment, you will interview an adult to discover signs of the seasons and write these season signs on a bingo card. **What signs will you find this season?**

Hypothesis: _____

Caution: When exploring outdoors, bring an adult for safety.

THE STEPS

1. Ask an adult to share 8 signs of the current season.

2. For winter, they might tell you about hibernation, plants with bare branches, snow, or long dark nights.

3. For spring, they might tell you about birds making nests, new leaves, rainy weather, or days getting longer.

4. For summer, they might tell you about baby animals, flowers that bloom, long sunny days, or the sun shining from directly overhead.

5. For fall, they might tell you about squirrels saving nuts, leaves turning colors, windy days, or days getting shorter.

6. Write each seasonal sign in a space on your bingo card.

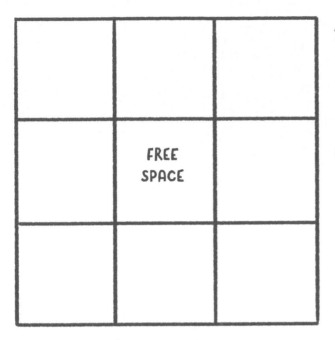

FREE SPACE

7. Go outside and search for the signs written on your bingo card! If you have a hand lens, magnifying glass, or binoculars, use your tools to see nature up close.

8. If you don't get a bingo today, keep your card nearby and continue adding to it throughout the season.

HOWS & WHYS: Because Earth's climate is changing, plants and animals get different temperature messages every year. Seasonal signs are different every year. For this reason, phenology is a science that needs people outdoors making **observations**. While we can guess what seasonal signs we will see based on what we remember from other years, thousands of citizen scientists observe and record phenology data for online databases.

(S)**(T)(E)(A)**(M) **Making great phenology observations often relies on technology, including tools for seeing things up close (like a magnifying glass or hand lens) or far away (like binoculars). Citizen scientists also use apps on their phones (like iNaturalist) that help them identify the creatures they discover.**

Now Try This!: Start a phenology journal. Find a blank notebook. Every day or week, record the temperature, weather, and any seasonal signs that you observe.

ROCKY ROAD

LEVEL OF DIFFICULTY:
MEDIUM
MESSY METER: MINOR MESS
FROM BEGINNING TO END:
1 HOUR
SEASONS:

MATERIALS

- ➲ Bucket, bag, or box for collecting rocks
- ➲ 1 penny (optional)
- ➲ Hand lens or magnifying glass (optional)

 Rocks can be **igneous**, **sedimentary**, or **metamorphic**. Igneous rocks form when molten rock, like lava, suddenly cools. Sedimentary rocks are made from layers of sand, mud, or other materials. Metamorphic rocks have been buried deep within the earth and changed by heat and pressure. **What kind of rocks can you find in your neighborhood?**

Hypothesis: ....

....

Caution: When exploring outdoors, bring an adult for safety.

THE STEPS

1. Go outdoors and look for rocks.

2. Good places to find rocks include beaches, riverbeds, riverbanks, and the bottoms of cliffs.

3. Collect at least 3 interesting rocks and get ready to discover what kind of rocks they are.

4. Scratch your rock with the penny or your fingernail and notice what happens to it.

5. Feel the rock's weight in your hands. Is it heavy? Light?

6. Look closely at your rock. Does it have big holes? Is it smooth? Is it hard with layers? Check the chart below. Do you see your rocks there?

Sedimentary rocks can have layers or many small pieces loosely stuck together.	Igneous rocks can have large crystals, no crystals, or large air holes.	Metamorphic rocks are very hard and can have wavy bands.
Conglomerate rocks are sedimentary rocks made out of many different pieces of gravel and sand that have become cemented together.	Granite is an igneous rock with large crystals.	Gneiss (pronounced "nice") is a **foliated** metamorphic rock. Granite turns into gneiss under high heat and pressure.

HOWS & WHYS: Sedimentary rocks are often crumbly because they are made of loose materials. Igneous rocks, which are made of molten rock that cooled slowly underground, have large crystals. Igneous rocks that cooled quickly have no crystals and look as smooth as glass. Igneous rocks that cooled from lava shooting into the air have big holes where the air bubbles popped. Metamorphic rocks have been squished under miles of heavy earth and often have wavy layers called foliation.

CONTINUED

(S) (T) (E) (A) (M) Rock scientists, or **geologists**, often use technology like magnifying glasses and chemical tests to help identify rocks. The hardness scale is a math tool used to identify rocks based on how hard they are.

Now Try This!: If you really love rocks, you will love making a rock box. A rock box is a collection of identified rocks arranged artfully in a container. You can use a shoebox and glue your rocks down in a cool pattern with their names written nearby.

A TRICKY CHOICE

LEVEL OF DIFFICULTY:

MEDIUM

MESSY METER:

MEDIUM MESS

FROM BEGINNING TO END:

1 HOUR

SEASONS:

MATERIALS

- Scissors
- 2 clear plastic cups
- Roll of tape
- Handful of wet leaves
- Handful of dry leaves
- Place to look for pill bugs

 Pill bugs, or roly-polies, are small **crustaceans**, shelled animals like crabs, that can roll into little balls. Pill bugs can be found in places with rotting vegetation, like under rocks and old leaves. *If you give pill bugs a choice between a wet environment and a dry one, which one will they choose?*

Hypothesis: ....

Caution: Although pill bugs do not spread disease, it's best to keep them outside and to wash your hands after handling them.

THE STEPS

1. Use the scissors to trim the cups so that they are about 1 inch (2.5 centimeters) tall.

2. Trim a small doorway (opening) in each cup.

3. Line up the cups so that the doorways meet.

4. Tape the cups together.

5. Place a few wet leaves in one cup.

6. Place a few dry leaves in the other cup.

7. Look for pill bugs under rocks and wet leaves. Gently collect 10 pill bugs.

CONTINUED

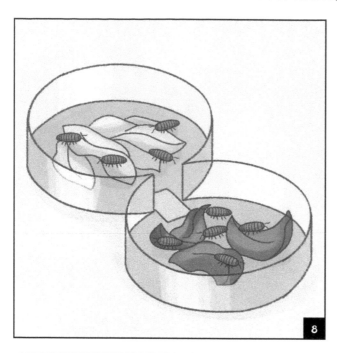

8. Place 5 pill bugs in 1 cup and 5 pill bugs in the other cup.

9. Watch the pill bugs for about 20 minutes. Given the choice between wet leaves and dry leaves, which do they choose? Count the number of pill bugs in each cup.

10. When you are finished with your experiment, gently put the pill bugs back where you found them.

HOWS & WHYS: Pill bugs need to stay wet. If a pill bug dries out, it will die. To stay alive, pill bugs will move toward wetter environments. This is why it is easier to find pill bugs in wet areas, like under wet leaves, than in dry environments, like in a sunny field. Many living things move toward water, food, light, or anything else that helps them stay alive.

S T E A M In this experiment, you used mechanical engineering skills to build a choice chamber. Choice chambers, like the two connected cups you made for this experiment, are a technology often used by scientists studying animals. Because you counted the pill bugs in each cup, you also used math.

Now Try This!: What other choices could you give your pill bugs? Brainstorm a list of choices you could set up in your choice chamber. For example, you could set up a sweet versus salty choice chamber with damp graham cracker in one cup and a damp salty cracker in the other cup. Or you could let the pill bugs choose between sand and soil.

HAPPY TRAILS

LEVEL OF DIFFICULTY:

MEDIUM

MESSY METER:

MEDIUM MESS

FROM BEGINNING TO END:

45 MINUTES

SEASONS:

MATERIALS

- 10 or more termites
- 1 Paper Mate brand ballpoint pen
- 2 pieces of paper
- Small paintbrush

Termites, like ants, are insects that work together. Because termites can't talk, they need other ways to communicate. Termites use chemical signals called **pheromones** to show one another where to go. Paper Mate brand pens use an ink that smells like pheromones to termites. ***Will it be easier for termites to follow a spiral ink trail, or a dotted-line ink trail?***

Hypothesis: ....

....

Caution: Termites should be studied outdoors and away from homes. If you order termites from a biological supply company, you can't release these bugs into the wild. Follow the disposal directions that come with the termites. Wash your hands after handling insects.

THE STEPS

1. Gather termites outdoors by searching under rotten wood, or order termites online from a biological supply company like Carolina Biological Supply (web address: Carolina.com). Use a paintbrush to gently pick up each insect separately.

2. Using the Paper Mate ballpoint pen, draw a straight dotted line on a piece of paper.

CONTINUED

3. Using the same pen, draw a spiral shape on a different piece of paper.

4. Use the paintbrush to gently place 5 termites at the beginning of the straight dotted line that you drew.

5. Use the paintbrush to gently place 5 termites at the beginning of the spiral that you drew.

6. Observe the movement of the termites. Count how many termites can stay on each line. Were there more termites that stayed on the straight dotted line or the spiral line?

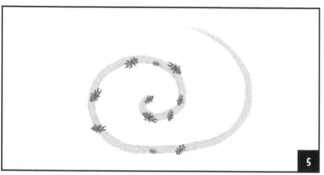

HOWS & WHYS: Most termites are blind and deaf. Termites smell pheromones with special feelers on their **antennae**. Termites use pheromone to share warnings about danger, to find their friends and family, and to organize trips to find food. Pheromone trails are chemical, not visual, so the shape of the line shouldn't make a difference to the termites. However, a broken line with spaces between the ink would be very difficult for termites to follow, because they would lose the scent of the trail.

S **T** F **A** M By creating patterns with ink, you exercised your art skills in this experiment. Because you counted the termites that could follow the trails, you also used math.

Now Try This!: Do you think that different colors of ink make trails with different scents? Try creating two identical patterns for the termites with red and blue Paper Mate pens.

COLD CLOUD

LEVEL OF DIFFICULTY:
MEDIUM

MESSY METER: MINOR MESS

FROM BEGINNING TO END:
20 MINUTES

SEASON:

when the temperature outside is –14°F (–26°C) or colder

MATERIALS

- ➔ 1-quart pot with lid
- ➔ About 2 cups of water
- ➔ Stove
- ➔ Oven mitt

 Water changes **phases**, from gas to liquid to solid, every day all around us. Ice cubes melt into puddles and boiling water steams. In very cold temperatures, water can change phases in an instant. ***Do you think you will get a better cloud from boiling water or warm water?***

Hypothesis: ....

....

Caution: Have an adult complete steps 5 to 8. Boiling water is very hot. Be careful to throw the water away and downwind.

THE STEPS

1. On a very cold winter day, bundle up in warm winter clothing.

2. Go outside and figure out which direction the wind is blowing. You will be throwing your water downwind so that the wind carries the water away from you.

3. Fill your pot about halfway full with about 2 cups of water.

4. Place the pot on the stove with the lid on the pot.

5. Have an adult turn on the stove and bring the water to a boil.

6. Once the water is boiling, have an adult turn the stove off.

CONTINUED

7. Have the adult carry the boiling water outside right away.

8. Have the adult take the lid off the pot and, holding the handle firmly, move the pot in a big arc from their waist upward, tossing the water out of the pot. They should be sure the water is tossed downwind.

9. Repeat step 8 with about 2 cups of warm water from the faucet.

10. Did the boiling water or the warm water make a bigger cloud?

HOWS & WHYS: When hot or warm water is very suddenly cooled, it condenses, changing from a gas (steam) to a liquid (water). This is only possible when the air is very cold, at least –14°F. The hotter the water is, the faster it condenses and the bigger the cloud. The big cloud that you see is made of many tiny drops of water. The clouds that you see in the sky are also made of many tiny drops of water. If you want to change your steam to a solid (snow), it has to be at least –42°F outside. *Brrr!*

⑤①①①⑩ Because you were comparing water of two different temperatures, you were doing math in this experiment. A stove is a tool, so technology was also involved.

Now Try This!: You can watch water change through all three phases: solid, liquid, and gas. Begin by filling a bowl with ice cubes. Leave the bowl on a table or the kitchen counter to let the ice cubes melt. Once all of the water in your bowl is liquid, pour it into a pot and ask an adult to help you boil it uncovered. The water will leave the pot and enter the air of your home in the gas phase (steam).

FLASHLIGHT TAG

LEVEL OF DIFFICULTY:
MEDIUM
MESSY METER: MINOR MESS
FROM BEGINNING TO END:
20 MINUTES
SEASONS:

MATERIALS

- A dark night
- A friend, sibling, or adult
- Flashlight

 The night sky is full of stars and **galaxies**. Stars are huge balls of burning gas. Galaxies are groups of many stars. Stars and galaxies are very bright. In this experiment, you will use a flashlight outside at night to explore light in the dark and to answer the question: **Why is the night sky dark?**

Hypothesis: _____

Caution: When you go outside at night, make sure an adult knows where you are or comes with you.

THE STEPS

1. Go outdoors on a dark night. Make sure that an adult knows where you are or comes with you.

2. One person is the observer. The other person holds the flashlight.

3. Both people should stand facing each other with space behind them.

4. The person with the flashlight should turn the flashlight on and point it toward the observer. Imagine that the flashlight is a star or galaxy. Notice how bright the flashlight is.

CONTINUED

5. The person with the flashlight should keep the flashlight pointed toward the observer while walking away. Notice that the flashlight becomes less bright as it gets farther away.

HOWS & WHYS: The universe is expanding in every direction. For this reason, all of the stars and galaxies that you can see from Earth are moving away from you. When objects move away from a person, the light they give off gets less and less bright. The light from some stars and galaxies is so dim that it is invisible to humans. These parts of the night sky appear dark.

S T E A M Building a model, or simple version, of a big event, is an important skill in both science and engineering. Astronomers are star scientists who use math to find stars and galaxies in our universe.

Now Try This!: Although it might seem like the night sky is holding still, there can be a lot of movement up there! Find your local astronomical society or do an Internet search of the term "Astronomy events near me" to find out when you can watch for moving planets, comets, meteor showers, aurora borealis (also called the "northern lights"), eclipses, equinoxes, solstices, and great views of the moon.

MYSTERIOUS WINTER TREES

LEVEL OF DIFFICULTY: HARD

MESSY METER: MINOR MESS

FROM BEGINNING TO END:
30 MINUTES

SEASON:

In spring, summer, and fall, look under the leaves for seeds and branching.

MATERIALS

- Trees
- Hand lens or magnifying glass (optional)

 The easiest way to identify a tree is to look at its leaves. In the winter, most trees don't have leaves. *What other tree parts might give you clues for identifying types of trees in winter?*

Hypothesis: ....

....

Caution: Be sure to have adult supervision whenever climbing trees.

THE STEPS

1. Begin by looking at the branches of a tree. Do the leaves look like needles? Or are they scaly and green? If the leaves are needlelike or scaly, the tree is **coniferous:** a pine, fir, spruce, juniper, cedar, cypress, yew, or redwood.

2. Notice if your tree has leaves on its branches and if there are needles on the ground under it. Larch and tamarack trees are conifers that drop their needlelike leaves in winter. If your tree has no leaves on its branches but needles on the ground, it is most likely one of these.

CONTINUED

acorn
(oak tree)

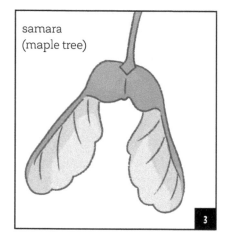

samara
(maple tree)

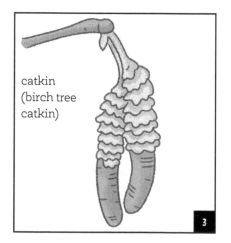

catkin
(birch tree
catkin)

3. If the tree has no leaves in the winter, it is **deciduous**. Look for seeds on the branches and on the ground. Use the illustrations to the left to match your tree's seeds to a tree name.

4. If the tree has no seeds, look at its branches. Use the illustration below to discover the type of branching.

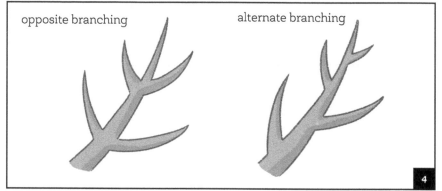

opposite branching   alternate branching

HOWS & WHYS: Seeds and branching patterns provide clues to identifying trees in the winter, because they are unique to certain groups of trees. Having particular seed types helps trees survive in their environments. Fewer types of trees have opposite branching patterns, so opposite branches can be a great clue.

S T E A M Comparing the shape, or form, of living things is a math skill. Many scientists use comparisons to help identify all kinds of living things.

Now Try This!: If you'd like to go deeper into the mystery of winter trees, consider exploring twigs, tree buds, and bark types.

EGGS-TREME HEAT

LEVEL OF DIFFICULTY: HARD
MESSY METER:
MEDIUM MESS
FROM BEGINNING TO END:
30 MINUTES (PLUS
1 HOUR IF USING
ALUMINUM FOIL)
SEASON:

MATERIALS

- 2 eggs
- Concrete sidewalk
- Asphalt road or empty parking lot
- Thermometer (optional)
- Frying pan or aluminum foil (optional)

? On a very hot day, people sometimes say, "It's hot enough to cook an egg on the sidewalk." America even has a National Fry an Egg on the Sidewalk Day (July 4). **On a very hot day, is an egg more likely to cook on a sidewalk or on an asphalt road?**

Hypothesis: _____

! Caution: Be certain to stay away from traffic when frying your egg on an asphalt road. Cleaning your egg off the sidewalk and road may be difficult, so consider setting out pieces of aluminum foil on top of your cooking spaces 1 hour before cracking your eggs.

THE STEPS

1. On a very hot summer day, bring 2 eggs outside.

2. Find a space on a concrete sidewalk that is in the sun. If you have a thermometer, measure the temperature of the air just above the sidewalk.

3. If you want an easy cleanup, set a frying pan or piece of aluminum foil on top of the sidewalk and let it heat up for 1 to 2 hours.

4. Crack an egg onto the sidewalk and watch it for 5 minutes. If the outside part of the egg starts to turn white, your egg is cooking.

CONTINUED

5. Find a space on an asphalt road or empty parking lot that is in the sun. If you have a thermometer, measure the temperature of the air just above the road.

6. If you want an easy cleanup, set a frying pan or a piece of aluminum foil on top of the asphalt road and let it heat up for 1 to 2 hours.

7. Crack an egg onto this area of the asphalt road and watch it for 5 minutes. Does it cook?

HOWS & WHYS: Eggs need to get to over 150°F (65°C) to begin to cook. Even the hottest places on Earth rarely get above 120°F (49°C). A sidewalk or parking lot is more likely to get hotter than the air around it if it is dark in color. Parking lot asphalt is a darker material than sidewalk concrete, so eggs are more likely to fry on asphalt than on a sidewalk.

S T E A M Because you were comparing temperatures in this experiment, you were using math. You will be doing some really cool chemical and mechanical engineering if you do "Now Try This!"

Now Try This!: In the town of Oatman, Arizona, participants in the annual sidewalk egg-frying contest build many different kinds of solar cookers to get higher temperatures to fry their eggs. How could you increase the heat of your sidewalk area to cook your egg more thoroughly? Try building a see-through dome with a glass or plastic cooking pot lid, concentrating solar heat with a large magnifying glass, or setting up an aluminum-foil mirror to trap heat over your egg-frying area.

ENLIGHTENING BUGS

LEVEL OF DIFFICULTY: HARD

MESSY METER:

MEDIUM MESS

FROM BEGINNING TO END:

20 MINUTES

SEASONS:

Bugs are usually more active in warm weather.

MATERIALS

→ Flashlight
→ Brown paper lunch bag

 When you go outside at night, you might notice bugs flying around outdoor lights. Some bugs always move toward light. Other bugs hide from light. **Do light-loving bugs like bright lights or low lights better?**

Hypothesis: _____

_____

Caution: When you go outside at night, make sure an adult knows where you are or comes with you.

THE STEPS

1. Go outside to a dark area and turn the flashlight on.

2. Point the flashlight at the ground.

3. For 5 minutes, count how many different bugs come up to the flashlight.

4. Turn the flashlight off. Wait 1 minute for all of the bugs to fly away.

5. Put the flashlight in the brown paper lunch bag and turn it on again. The light should be much less bright.

6. Point the flashlight at the ground.

7. For 5 minutes, count how many different bugs come up to the flashlight.

CONTINUED

8. Did more bugs come to the bright light or the dim light?

HOWS & WHYS: Bugs like light, and the brighter the light, the more they like it. Bright lights can be seen from farther away and will attract more bugs. Scientists think that light-loving bugs might use the light of the sun or moon to find their way around. Human-made lamps confuse bugs, and they end up flying in circles. Some bugs might confuse lights for flowers.

⑤①ⒺⒶⓂ Using a brown paper lunch bag to change the brightness of a flashlight is an example of engineering. Because you counted and compared the bugs that flew to each light, you also did math.

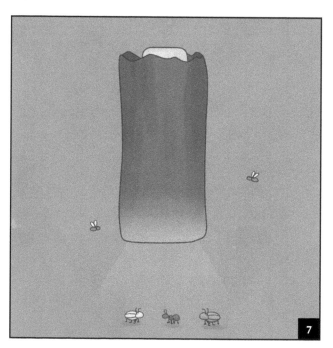

Now Try This!: You can change the color of light coming out of a flashlight by covering it with color plastic wrap or cellophane. Experiment with different colors of light to see what colors attract the most bugs.

SPOTLIGHT ON: ENVIRONMENTAL SCIENTISTS!

Environmental scientists apply their knowledge of science to study and protect the environment and human health. Clean water, clean air, healthy forests, plentiful schools of fish, and strong herds of bison are just a few of the benefits that we enjoy because of the work of environmental scientists. They might spend their days scuba diving in rivers to protect endangered water creatures, digging deep into the ground to find hidden pollution, or conducting chemical tests in labs to measure how safe water sources are to drink. If you love doing science outdoors, you may want to become an environmental scientist one day so that you can protect and conserve the natural resources and places that make our planet a fantastic place to live.

Chapter Three

TECHNOLOGY

Technology is connected to the outdoors in lots of ways. There are many tech tools that help scientists learn about the outdoors. Also, inventions are often inspired by the outdoors. For example, Velcro was inspired by hooks in seeds that attach to animal fur (and the clothes of people who walk through patches of sticker plants!). Finally, when nature itself cannot provide for our needs, technologies fill in. For example, technologies such as hydroponics and fertilizers make it possible for us to have enough food to eat in places where the weather is too cold or the soil does not have enough nutrients for food to grow naturally.

In this chapter, you will build and use a variety of outdoor tools, often with materials found in nature. As you learn how to measure rain, purify water, and tell time without a clock, think about how humans have been building and improving technologies since ancient times.

RAIN GAUGE

LEVEL OF DIFFICULTY: EASY

MESSY METER:

MEDIUM MESS

FROM BEGINNING TO END:

30 MINUTES

SEASONS:

In most parts of the United States, more rain falls in the spring and summer.

MATERIALS

- 2 clear glass jars or plastic bottles
- Scissors
- Ruler
- Permanent marker
- Rocks or gravel
- 2 outdoor areas for the rain gauge: 1 on pavement and 1 on grass

? Weather scientists, or **meteorologists**, use many technologies to measure and predict weather events like rain and snow. In this experiment, you will build a meteorologist tool called a **rain gauge** to measure how much rain falls during a rainstorm. ***Do you think that more rain will fall on pavement or on grass?***

Hypothesis: ....

....

THE STEPS

1. If you are using glass jars, skip this step. If you are using plastic bottles, have an adult cut off the tapering tops so that both bottles become even cylinders.

2. Hold the ruler up to your jar or bottle. Using the permanent marker, begin at the bottom and draw a horizontal line on the container for every inch (centimeter).

3. Go outside and find a few rocks or a handful of gravel to place in the bottom of your rain gauges. This will anchor your rain gauges to the ground.

4. Place 1 rain gauge on the pavement and the other on grass.

5. Check your rain gauge after the next rainstorm. How many inches (centimeters) of rain are in each of your rain gauges?

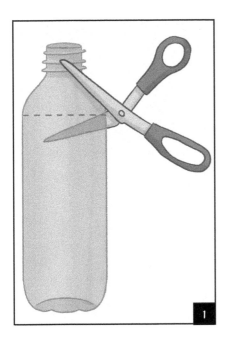

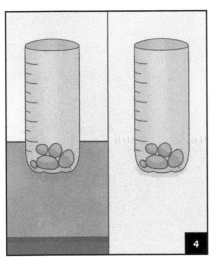

HOWS & WHYS: A rain gauge works by catching the rain or snow that falls during a rainstorm or snowstorm. The height of the water in the rain gauge is the amount of water that falls in the storm. The same amount of water falls on pavement and on grass, but because water can't be **absorbed** by pavement the way it can by grass, it may seem like more rain falls on pavement.

S T E A M Meteorologists use many different technologies, including thermometers to measure temperature, barometers to measure air pressure, and anemometers to measure wind. Meteorologists use math and science to understand the information they get from their tools, just like you used math and science to understand the amount of rain in your rainstorm.

Now Try This!: Think about the different outdoor habitats near your home. Will the same amount of water fall in a forest and in a grassland? Test the amount of rain that falls in the different habitats you can visit.

HOME HYDROPONICS

LEVEL OF DIFFICULTY:
MEDIUM
MESSY METER: MINOR MESS
FROM BEGINNING TO END:
20 MINUTES, PLUS SHORT
OBSERVATIONS OVER
1 TO 2 WEEKS
SEASONS:

Hydroponics is a way of growing plants without soil. Instead of planting seeds in dirt, hydroponic farmers and gardeners plant seeds in water, adding special chemicals to provide the **nutrients** plants need. In this experiment, you will try sprouting seeds with hydroponic technology to answer the question: **How do plants grow without soil?**

Hypothesis: ....

....

MATERIALS

- 1 paper towel or 2 coffee filters
- 1 plastic zip-top bag
- Water
- 5 dried beans or untreated, plain popcorn kernels
- Tape or string

THE STEPS

1. Fold 1 paper towel or 2 coffee filters so that they will take up about half of the space in your zip-top bag.

2. Take the paper towel out of the zip-top bag and dampen it with water.

3. Squeeze the water out of the paper towel so that it is just damp, but not dripping wet. (A dripping-wet paper towel will grow mold.)

4. Put the damp paper towel back into the zip-top bag.

5. Slide 5 beans or corn kernels in between the zip-top bag and the paper towel so that you can see the seed from the outside of the bag.

6. Place the bag in a warm, sunny place. Most seeds need temperatures at 65°F (18°C) to sprout. In the winter, you can tape your bag to the inside of a window. In warmer seasons, you can tape your bag to the outside of a window or tie it to the trunk of a tree.

7. Watch your seeds sprout by checking on them daily for 1 to 2 weeks. Describe what is happening to a sibling, friend, or adult, or draw pictures to record your observations.

HOWS & WHYS: Seeds need warmth and water to sprout. Once the seeds are sprouted into plants, they also need light, air, nutrients, and support. As long as all of these needs are met, plants can grow without soil. Farmers who use hydroponics can grow food in places and seasons when outdoor soil isn't available.

Ⓢ Ⓣ Ⓔ Ⓐ Ⓜ Hydroponics applies **botany**, the science of plants, to grow plants without soil. Farmers use math to calculate the amount of nutrients that they will add to the water given to their hydroponic crops. In this experiment, you can also use art to organize or decorate your seed-starting bag.

CONTINUED

NOW TRY THIS!

Now Try This!: If you enjoyed sprouting seeds with hydroponics, you can keep going by building a larger hydroponic planter for your bean or corn plants. Cut the top off a large plastic bottle and set it aside. Fill the bottom of the bottle with water and a few drops of fertilizer. Place the top of the bottle that you cut off back in the bottle, upside down. Then dampen a piece of paper towel, bunch it up, tie a string around the bottom of it, and stuff it into the upside-down top with the string dangling down. Fill the bottom of the bottle with water and a few drops of fertilizer, and watch your plant grow!

FERTILIZER FUN

LEVEL OF DIFFICULTY:
MEDIUM
MESSY METER:
MEDIUM MESS
FROM BEGINNING TO END:
30 MINUTES FOR PLANT
SETUP, WITH 10-MINUTE
ACTIVITIES FOR 2 WEEKS
SEASONS:

MATERIALS

- An outdoor area with 6 plants of the same kind, like a garden
- 1 small container (1 quart or less) indoor or outdoor liquid chemical fertilizer
- Bucket
- 1 small bucket or bag of compost (You can use compost from your own yard if your family keeps a compost pile, or you can find it at your free city compost site. It's also available at hardware and home supply stores.)
- Water

Agronomists are scientists who add exactly the right amount of nutrients to soil so that farm crops will grow better. In this experiment, you will test chemical and organic fertilizers to see how they help plants grow. **Will chemical fertilizers or organic compost help plants grow more?**

Hypothesis: ....

Caution: Never eat fertilizer.

THE STEPS

1. Go outside and find a group of 6 plants that are the same. You could pick bushes, grass, or garden plants.

2. Read the directions on the liquid chemical fertilizer bottle. Follow the directions to prepare one bucket of water with fertilizer. Pour this fertilizer water over 3 of your plants.

3. Place one handful of compost on the soil surrounding the stems of the other 3 plants. (Do not get compost on the plants' leaves.) Pour a bucket of water over the compost.

4. Observe your plants every day for 2 weeks. Notice the color of their leaves, the strength of their stems, and their overall shape. Do any new leaves grow?

CONTINUED

5. If it does not rain for 3 or more days, repeat steps 2 and 3 every day until it rains.

6. At the end of 2 weeks, compare the chemically fertilized plants with the composted plants. Is there a difference?

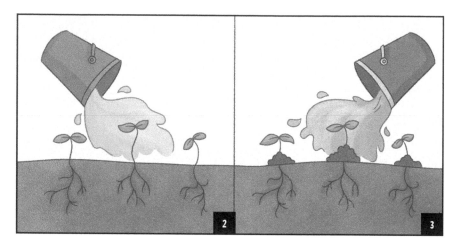

HOWS & WHYS: Earth's soils can be very different. On some farms, nature can provide many of the nutrients that crop plants need to grow. On other farms, fertilizer technologies are needed to grow food. Agronomists usually work with chemical fertilizers that cost a lot of money. Knowing whether it's better to use chemical fertilizer or compost involves measuring the nutrients in the soil and making a plan to keep the farmland healthy in the future.

S T E A M Botany, the science of plants, helps farmers and agronomists know what kinds of nutrients plants need. Soil science is also involved when agronomists measure nutrients.

Now Try This!: In this experiment, you used 3 plants to test chemical fertilizer and 3 plants to test compost. They were all the same kind of plant, and they were growing in the same area. In this experiment, the number of plants, kind of plants, and location of plants were **controls**. Scientists use controls to make sure that outside factors don't change the results of their experiments. Can you redesign this experiment with even more controls, like the temperature of the plants or the amount of water they get?

SOLAR STILL

LEVEL OF DIFFICULTY:
MEDIUM
MESSY METER:
MEDIUM MESS
FROM BEGINNING TO END:
1 HOUR TO BUILD, PLUS
1 TO 2 DAYS FOR THE
WATER TO COLLECT
SEASONS:

MATERIALS

- Shovel
- Outdoor area where you can dig a large hole (1 foot wide by 1 foot deep)
- Ruler
- 1 (2-inch-wide) small jar with lid
- Handful of grass clippings or fallen leaves (optional)
- Bucket of water
- Clear plastic tarp or plastic wrap (3 feet wide by 3 feet long)

 Energy from the sun, or **solar** energy, can be used to make electricity, to heat buildings, and even to give us drinking water in places where there isn't any. A solar **still** is an invention that uses the sun's energy to heat, boil, and collect pure water from an undrinkable water source. **How can the sun's energy be used to clean water?**

Hypothesis: ....

....

Caution: Do not drink water from your solar still.

THE STEPS

1. After getting permission, use your shovel to dig a hole that is 1 foot wide and 1 foot deep. Dig a little hole, about 2 inches (5 centimeters) deep, in the center of the bigger hole. Measure with your ruler.

2. Place the small jar in the little hole. Keep the lid on it for now.

3. If you have grass clippings or fallen leaves, pile these around the jar. This will provide extra water for your still.

4. Pour 1 bucketful of water over the grass clippings in the big hole, working around the jar.

5. Take the lid off the jar.

⚫TⒺⒶⓂ In this experiment, you used mechanical engineering to build a solar still. You also used the science of the water cycle to power your technology.

6. Cover the big hole with a clear plastic tarp or plastic wrap. Use rocks to hold the tarp down at the edges of the hole. Place a handful of dirt or a small rock in the middle of the tarp so that it dips down over the jar.

7. Come back in 1 to 2 days. The water in your jar has been **distilled**, or boiled and condensed, and should be clean. Just to be on the safe side, don't drink it!

HOWS & WHYS: When water is heated, it boils and becomes steam. This process is called **evaporation** and is an important part of Earth's water cycle. Water can evaporate out of soil and plants. In your solar still, the water that evaporated out of the soil and leaves was trapped by the tarp. Under the tarp, the water then went through a process called **condensation**, turning from steam back into liquid. That water dripped off the tarp and into the jar, leaving behind the dirt and bugs that were in the water in the soil and leaves.

CONTINUED

Now Try This!: Many places on Earth have plenty of salt water but don't have clean drinking water. Try setting up a solar still using a large bowl of salt water. Place an empty jar in the middle of the bowl and cover the whole bowl with plastic wrap. Water will evaporate out of the salt water, condense on the plastic wrap, and drip into the jar.

SUNNY DAZE

LEVEL OF DIFFICULTY:
MEDIUM

MESSY METER: MINOR MESS

FROM BEGINNING TO END:
7 (5-MINUTE) WORK
SESSIONS SPREAD OUT
OVER 6 HOURS

SEASONS:

MATERIALS

- 1 big stick
- Sunny outdoor area
- 5 medium
  rocks (optional)
- 1 (3-inch) ball of
  clay (optional)
- Clock
- 1 piece of sidewalk chalk
  or 12 small rocks

 Two hundred years ago (and earlier!) most people told time with sundials. A **sundial** is an outdoor clock that uses the movement of the sun through the sky to tell time. In this experiment, you will use outdoor materials to build a sundial. ***How do you think the sun will move through the sky?***

Hypothesis: ....
....

Caution: Never look directly at the sun.

THE STEPS

1. Before 9:00 a.m., set up a big stick in a sunny area so that the stick points vertically up to the sky. If you are working in a garden or park, you can push the stick in to the ground. If you are working in a paved area, you can use rocks to build a support for your stick or press your stick into a ball of clay.

2. At 9:00 a.m., use sidewalk chalk or rocks to mark where the stick's shadow falls.

3. Every hour until 3:00 p.m., mark where the stick's shadow falls. Label each mark with the hour.

4. You now have a sundial! Tomorrow, the stick will cast the same shadows at the same times. You can look at where the stick's shadow falls, and you will know what time it is without looking at a clock.

CONTINUED

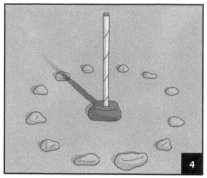

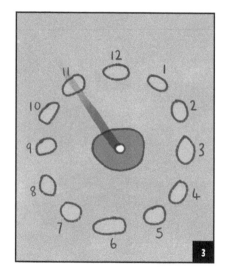

HOWS & WHYS: The sun moves through the sky in a similar path every day because Earth revolves around the sun in the same path every day. Although the path changes with the seasons, the difference in where the shadows fall barely changes from one day to the next.

S T E A M Sundials are an example of an ancient technology that uses the science of the seasons and solar system as well as mechanical engineering. Sundials can also be beautiful works of art.

Now Try This!: Make a permanent sundial for your home. Begin by filling a circular plastic container, 1 inch (2.5 centimeters) deep and at least 6 inches (15 centimeters) across, with clay. Smooth the clay flat. Use the sundial positions you discovered in this experiment to mark the clay with the hours of the day with small pebbles or beads. Press 9 pebbles or beads into the place where the shadow will fall at 9:00 a.m., 10 beads for 10:00 a.m., and so on. Place a stick or metal or wooden dowel in the center of the clay. Let your sundial dry and set it in a sunny area.

COOL COMPOST

LEVEL OF DIFFICULTY:
MEDIUM
MESSY METER:
MEDIUM MESS
FROM BEGINNING TO END:
30 MINUTES TO
SET UP, PLUS DAILY
OBSERVATIONS FOR
2 TO 4 WEEKS
SEASONS:

MATERIALS

- ➲ 2 (1-gallon) plastic milk jugs, 2 (2-liter) plastic bottles, or 2 buckets
- ➲ 1¼ gallons soil from outdoors (not packaged soil)
- ➲ 1 ruler
- ➲ 1 quart grass clippings or green leaves
- ➲ 1 quart brown leaves
- ➲ 1 quart plant-based food scraps, like fruit and vegetable peelings and coffee grounds
- ➲ Water
- ➲ 1 thermometer

Every year, leaves, petals, fruits, and nuts fall to the ground. All of these things disappear over time because of the magic of compost. In this experiment, you will use the technology of composting to make food scraps disappear. **When compost disappears, where does it go?**

Hypothesis: ....

....

Caution: Always wash your hands after handling compost.

THE STEPS

1. If using milk jugs or plastic bottles, have an adult cut the tops off.

2. Choose one container to be the control. Fill this container with soil from outdoors, leaving 3 inches (7.5 centimeters) of space at the top.

3. In the bottom of the other container, begin your compost with a layer of soil, about 1 inch (2.5 centimeters).

4. Add grass clippings or green leaves as well as brown leaves and food scraps to the compost container. Leave about 4 inches (10 centimeters) of space at the top.

CONTINUED

5. Top off the compost container with about 1 inch (2.5 centimeters) of soil.

6. Add ½ to 1½ cups of water to each container so that the soil is moist but not wet.

7. Place both containers in a sunny place.

8. Every day for 2 to 4 weeks, check your compost. Measure the temperature in both containers. Look for signs of change. Mix your compost daily so that air enters the container.

9. Repeat until the food scraps have turned into soil.

HOWS & WHYS: Soil is full of tiny creatures that break down materials, like leaves, by eating them. In your container, soil creatures broke down the food scraps, turning it into compost. This process also makes heat, just like your body makes heat when you break down the food that you eat. Big compost piles get really hot on the inside—as hot as 150°F (65°C)!

S T E A M Composting is a technology that lets farmers use the science of biology and chemical engineering to make soil rich and fertile without adding expensive chemical fertilizers.

Now Try This!: Set up a composting pile so that all of your family's food scraps are broken down into rich garden soil. Define the area with a box, wooden frame, or a compost bin that you buy at a hardware store, garden supply store, or home supply store. Be sure to add soil, grass clippings or green leaves, brown leaves, and food scraps. Stir your compost at least once a week with a pitchfork or shovel. When your compost looks like soil, you can add it to the soil in your garden to help your plants grow.

CLOUDY PREDICTIONS

LEVEL OF DIFFICULTY:
MEDIUM
MESSY METER: MINOR MESS
FROM BEGINNING TO END:
30 MINUTES
SEASONS:

MATERIALS

➔ **None**

? Meteorologists use many tools to **predict** the weather. One of the most important tricks to knowing what weather is coming is hidden in the clouds. A cloud chart is a tool that shows what kind of weather can be predicted by different kinds of clouds. **What kind of weather will the clouds bring today?**

Hypothesis: ....

....

THE STEPS

1. Go outdoors and lie down on the ground.

2. Take your time looking at the clouds.

3. Are they low to the earth or high in the sky?

4. Are the clouds piled up in thick stacks, or wispy and thin?

5. What color are the clouds? Are they light or dark?

6. Use the chart to figure out what kind of clouds are in the sky, and what kind of weather those clouds might bring.

> **HOWS & WHYS:** Earth is surrounded by a bubble of air. This air is always swirling and flowing in **currents**, areas in the sky with strong winds that are like rivers of air. Clouds ride on the air currents like boats on rivers high above Earth. The shape and height of clouds predict what weather the air currents will bring.

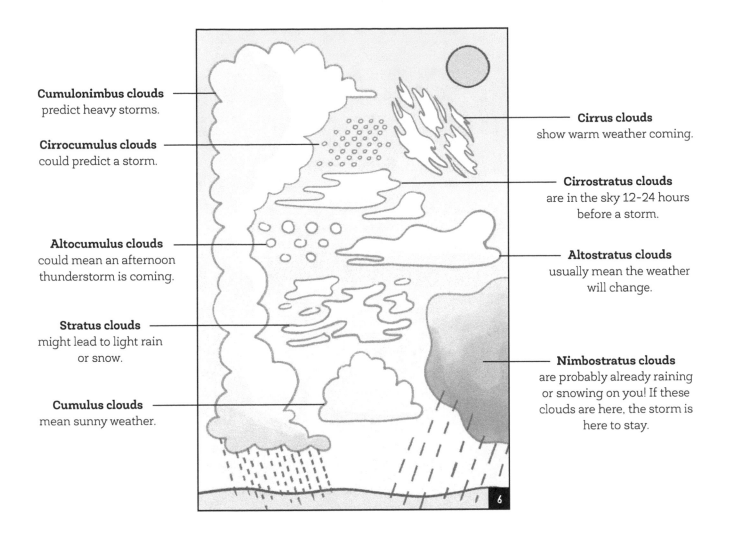

Cumulonimbus clouds predict heavy storms.

Cirrocumulus clouds could predict a storm.

Altocumulus clouds could mean an afternoon thunderstorm is coming.

Stratus clouds might lead to light rain or snow.

Cumulus clouds mean sunny weather.

Cirrus clouds show warm weather coming.

Cirrostratus clouds are in the sky 12-24 hours before a storm.

Altostratus clouds usually mean the weather will change.

Nimbostratus clouds are probably already raining or snowing on you! If these clouds are here, the storm is here to stay.

S T E A M Cloud charts are a kind of technology that includes art in the form of cloud drawings. Cloud charts also involve weather science.

Now Try This!: If you know clouds, you can help the National Aeronautics and Space Administration (NASA) collect important weather information. Do an Internet search of the words "NASA GLOBE Cloud" and you will find a link for submitting cloud data to NASA.

SINKING TEMPERATURES

LEVEL OF DIFFICULTY: HARD

MESSY METER:
MEDIUM MESS

FROM BEGINNING TO END:
1 TO 2 HOURS

SEASONS:

MATERIALS

- 3 clear jars or cups
- Handful of sand or gravel
- Cold and warm water
- Thermometer
- 1 small (2- to 4-ounce) plastic food storage container or 1 clean, empty film canister

? To measure temperatures, there is an ancient technology called a Galileo thermometer. A Galileo thermometer is a container of water with several small containers that float or sink, depending on the temperature of the water. In this experiment, you will build a basic Galileo thermometer, answering the question: **Will a container sink in cold water and float in warm water, or float in cold water and sink in warm water?**

Hypothesis: ....

....

THE STEPS

1. Use one of the cups to collect a handful of sand or gravel from outdoors.

2. Fill the second cup with cold water and the third cup with warm water. You can fill both cups with water from an outdoor hose. Leave one cup in the shade to stay cool and the other in the sun to warm up for 30 minutes (if it's summer). Or, you can use the cold and warm water from an indoor faucet.

3. Fill an empty plastic food storage container about ¼ full of sand or gravel and snap on the lid.

4. Drop the food storage container into the cold water, and then the warm water. If it floats in both containers, take it out and add a little more sand or gravel.

5. Keep adding sand in small amounts until the food storage container sinks in the cold water and floats in the warm water.

6. Take the temperature of the cold water and the warm water.

7. The cold temperature is the temperature at which your food storage container will sink in water.

8. The warm temperature is the temperature at which your food storage container will float in water.

9. Try leaving your food storage container in a bucket of water outdoors for a few days. If it sinks, you'll know that the temperature is the same as the cold water in your cup. If it floats, you'll know that the temperature is the same as the warm water in the other cup. If it neither floats nor sinks, you'll know that the temperature is somewhere in between.

CONTINUED

HOWS & WHYS: Density is a measurement of how much space something takes up in relation to how much matter, or material, is in it. Some objects will sink or float no matter what. But some objects have a density that is very close to the density of water. Because the density of water changes when it is hot or cold, these objects can sink or float depending on temperature.

(S) (T) (E) (A) (M) **When you explored density, you were applying math and science in order to build your technology.**

Now Try This!: To take this experiment to the next level, build a full Galileo thermometer. Use a permanent marker to label the food storage container with the temperature of the cold water in which it sank. Repeat this experiment with many different temperatures of water until you have 5 to 10 food storage containers labeled with different temperatures. Place your labeled food storage containers in a clear container outside and use it to measure temperature.

HEAT OR HUMIDITY?

LEVEL OF DIFFICULTY: HARD

MESSY METER: MINOR MESS

FROM BEGINNING TO END:
1 HOUR

SEASONS:

MATERIALS

- 2 inexpensive alcohol thermometers
- 3 rubber bands
- 1 stick, at least 2 feet (30 centimeters) long and at least 1 inch (2.5 centimeters) thick
- A few drops of water
- Small piece of gauze or cloth, about 1 inch (2.5 centimeters) square

 Have you ever noticed that wet weather feels different from dry weather, even when the thermometer shows the same temperature? In this experiment, you will build a tool called a sling psychrometer, or hygrometer, that meteorologists use to measure how much water is in the air. **Do you think that wet air will be hotter or colder than dry air?**

Hypothesis: ....

....

Caution: Never use a mercury thermometer.

THE STEPS

1. Place the thermometers on opposite sides of one end of the stick.

2. Use rubber bands to hold the thermometers in place.

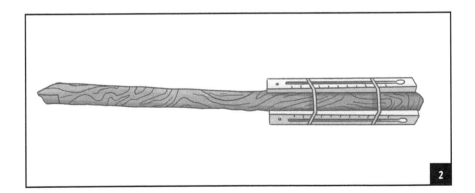

CONTINUED

3. Use a few drops of water to get a small piece of cloth damp but not dripping wet.

4. Use a rubber band to place the cloth over the bulb at the bottom of one of the thermometers.

5. Hold the stick firmly and draw a circle in the air with your arm extended. Keep circling your arm for 1 minute.

6. Quickly check both thermometers and notice the different temperatures. Did the wet thermometer give a hotter or colder reading than the dry thermometer?

HOWS & WHYS: A hot, dry summer day feels very different from a hot, sticky summer day. When the air is full of water, we say that the weather is humid. Humid weather in the summer feels so hot that people sometimes say, "It's not the heat, it's the humidity." In hot humid weather, the sweat we make can't evaporate off our skin and cool us, so the temperature feels hotter than usual. In cold humid weather, the air pulls heat from our bodies more quickly, and the temperature feels colder than usual.

(S) **T** (E) **A** (M) **In this experiment, you used engineering to build your tool. Because you were comparing temperatures and humidity, you also used math.**

Now Try This!: You can check for humidity with a glass of ice water. Just set out a glass of water with 4 to 5 ice cubes and wait for about 10 minutes. If the outside of the glass gets wet, this means that the air has lots of water in it—enough to condense on the outside of the glass, just like water droplets condense in clouds!

STAR DIRECTIONS

LEVEL OF DIFFICULTY: HARD

MESSY METER:

MEDIUM MESS

FROM BEGINNING TO END:

1 HOUR

SEASONS:

MATERIALS

- Flashlight
- 1 red bottle cap (that will fit over the flashlight) or red cellophane
- Small strip of folded paper (optional)
- 1 rubber band (optional)
- Dark, open area for viewing the stars
- 4 to 8 rocks, sticks, or other natural place markers

A **compass** is a tool used for finding the **cardinal directions**—north, south, east, and west—which is very helpful for reading maps and finding directions in the wilderness. A compass has a magnetic needle that always points north when mounted on top of a **compass rose**, a diagram showing the cardinal directions. **Can you find north outdoors by using a handmade compass?**

Hypothesis: _____

_____

Caution: When you go outside at night, make sure an adult knows where you are or comes with you.

THE STEPS

1. Before you go stargazing, you will need to make a red light. A red light lets you look at your star chart while keeping your eyes adjusted to the dark, so that you can also find stars.

2. Fit a red bottle cap over your flashlight. If your cap is a little bit too big for your flashlight, you can line the bottle cap with a small strip of folded paper to fill in the gap. Or use a rubber band to secure 3 to 4 layers of red cellophane over your flashlight.

CONTINUED

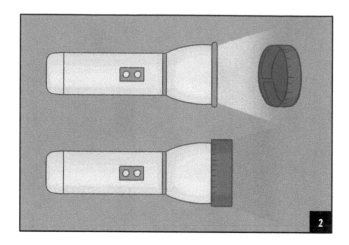

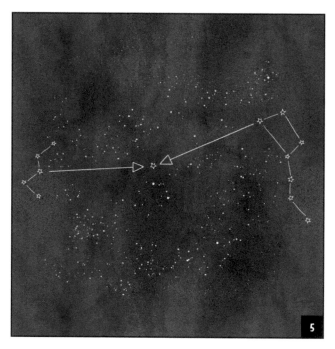

3. Go outside at night to an open area. Find a secure seat and look up. Use the star chart and your view of the sky to find the Big Dipper.

4. Imagine a line running up from the bottom of the Big Dipper. This line will point directly at Polaris, also known as the North Star.

5. You can also find Polaris by finding the star in the middle of the constellation Cassiopeia, which points toward Polaris.

6. Stand facing Polaris and set a natural place marker, like a rock or stick, on or in the ground directly in front of you. This is north on your compass rose.

7. Point your right hand out to your side. This is east on your compass rose. Place another rock or stick on or in the ground, the same distance as your north place marker, but to the east.

8. Repeat this process to mark west to your left and south behind you.

9. Now whenever you come to your stargazing place, you will know all of the cardinal directions.

HOWS & WHYS: Polaris never seems to move in the night sky because Earth's axis points directly at Polaris. Polaris is directly over Earth's North Pole. Therefore, if you point toward Polaris, you are pointing toward the cardinal direction of north.

Ⓢ Ⓣ Ⓔ Ⓐ Ⓜ In this experiment, you used engineering to build your red light. You used the science of astronomy to locate Polaris. Because you created a compass rose, you also used art.

Now Try This!: Try using natural materials to build an outdoor map of your home and several local landmarks. For example, your home could be a mini building made of sticks, and a local river could be braided grass. Use your stargazing skills to include a compass rose in your map.

SPOTLIGHT ON: HYDROLOGISTS!

Hydrologists are scientists who study water. When you think about the fact that 71 percent of Earth's surface is covered with water, it's easy to see why the work of hydrologists is so important. When hydrologists work to make sure that people have access to clean water or to stop flooding during extreme weather events, they use really cool technology. Stream gauges measure how fast water flows. Satellites can be equipped with **infrared** (heat-sensing) cameras to measure water temperature across the globe. Although hydrologists use computers to analyze and understand their data, they also work outdoors, collecting samples from lakes, rivers, oceans, and even glaciers. Hydrology is a popular career, so if you love technology and studying water, this may be a great option for your future.

Chapter Four

ENGINEERING

Engineering makes it possible for humans to live in harmony with the outdoors. The experiments in this chapter include several **mechanical engineering** challenges. One experiment is inspired by some of nature's best builders: beavers. You will also learn how to build structures out of sand and ice.

Environmental engineering brings together knowledge from many different types of science to make solutions that help keep our planet and the creatures that live here healthy. In this chapter, you will explore engineering solutions that predict weather, keep water clean, and help farms produce food. You will also get to learn from nature, studying bubbles to learn about physics and creating nature-inspired inventions.

The experiments in this chapter will give you opportunities to try **engineering design**, a cycle that involves finding a problem, creating and testing solutions, and retesting solutions so that they work even better. It's important to remember that failure is part of engineering design. If your first design doesn't work, you can learn from the experience. Don't give up! Keep engineering to create even better solutions.

BEAVER DAM

LEVEL OF DIFFICULTY: EASY

MESSY METER:

MEDIUM MESS

FROM BEGINNING TO END:

30 MINUTES

SEASONS:

 How do beavers build a dam?

Hypothesis: ....
....

 Caution: Make sure an adult is with you, because you'll be playing with water.

MATERIALS

- Small riverbed (This can be a natural stream, a sandbox or sandy area, tub, or sink. If you are building indoors in a sink or a tub, stones, leaves, or aluminum foil can be used to make a streambed.)
- 10 to 20 sticks
- 10 to 20 stones
- 10 to 20 leaves
- Water source (This can be a natural stream, a garden hose, a bucket of water, or, if working inside at a tub or sink, a faucet.)
- A pile of mud

THE STEPS

1. Set up a riverbed. You can use a natural stream or build your own. To build your own, make a path for a river with stones, leaves, or aluminum foil.

2. Pour water into the top of the streambed and keep adding water until it reaches the end. Notice how the water flows through.

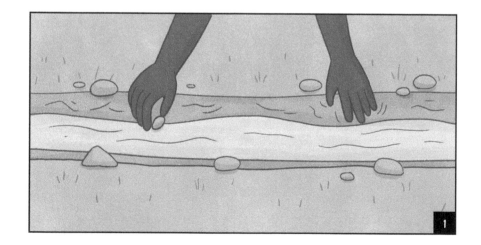

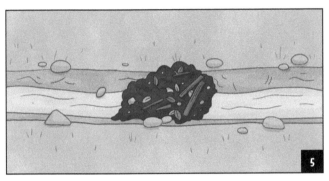

3. Use sticks, stones, leaves, and mud to build a dam that will stop the water from flowing.

4. Test your beaver dam by pouring water into the top of the streambed and noticing where the water goes. Does the dam stop the water?

5. Use more sticks, leaves, and mud to rebuild your dam and test it again.

HOWS & WHYS: Beavers are nature's engineers. Their dams change the flow of water in nature, building lakes and ponds that many plants and animals call home. When beavers build dams, they use sticks to frame the dam. Stones weigh it down. Leaves and mud fill in the cracks so that water doesn't leak out.

S T E A M In this mechanical engineering challenge, you used science when you tested your dam.

Now Try This!: Have you ever wondered how the dams engineered by humans make electricity? The water held back by a dam is full of energy because gravity wants to pull the water down the river. To see this in your dam, poke a hole and watch how quickly the water pours out of the hole.

IGLOO SLOOSH

LEVEL OF DIFFICULTY: EASY

MESSY METER: MINOR MESS

FROM BEGINNING TO END:
30 MINUTES

SEASON:

MATERIALS

- Ice (If you are building in winter, gather ice from outside. In other seasons, ice cubes can be used.)
- Snow or slush (If there is no snow outside, you can make your own slush. Have an adult pulse 12 ice cubes in a blender until you have a slushy mixture. You may need to make more than one batch of slush to build your igloo.)
- Pie tin (if you are building inside) (optional)
- Spoon (optional)

? An **igloo** is a house made from blocks of snow. Inuit people in the US, Canada, and Greenland engineer small igloos as camping shelters for hunting trips, and historically have even engineered larger igloos for homes. Only some types of snow are helpful for building igloos. In this experiment, you will build an icy igloo to explore the question: **Can slush and snow glue blocks of ice together?**

Hypothesis: ....

....

! **Caution:** Ice is very cold. Be careful when handling it. Snow is not safe to eat.

THE STEPS

1. Place pieces of ice in a circle, nestled into snow on the ground or on a layer of slush in a pie tin.

2. Fill the inside of the ice circle with a layer of snow or slush to hold the ice pieces in place. Add more slush on top of the ice to fill in any gaps or cracks.

3. Try to build a wall of ice by stacking more ice pieces on top of your first ice circle. Do they fall off? The slush in the middle of the circle should hold your bottom layer of ice cubes steady, so that you can stack more ice cubes on top. You might need to add slush between layers of ice cubes to help them stick together.

4. Add handfuls of snow or slush on top of your first ice circle, then try building your ice wall again. If you are building your igloo indoors, you might need to put it in the freezer for a few minutes if it starts to melt.

> **HOWS & WHYS:** Two ice cubes will not stick together without slush, because they are frozen solid. When melty snow or slush comes between the ice cubes, the ice will begin to freeze the snow or slush, and the ice will start to stick together.

S T E A M **Making igloos combines mechanical engineering and chemical engineering. When you applied knowledge of melting and freezing, you used science. Creating a building also involves architecture, the art and science of designing buildings.**

Now Try This!: Igloos are dome-shaped structures. For an advanced experiment, continue building your ice wall higher and connect all of the sides in a rounded roof. You may need to put your igloo in the freezer multiple times to keep it frozen.

CASTLES FOREVER

 To engineer a sandcastle, you need sticky sand. In this experiment, you will mix different amounts of water and sand to find the stickiest mixture. **What do you predict will be the stickiest mixture: 1 cup of sand with ¼, ⅓, ½, or 1 cup of water?**

Hypothesis: _____

Caution: When working with sand, avoid rubbing your eyes.

MATERIALS

- Bucket of sand (about 4 cups), from a beach, riverbank, playground, or sandbox
- 4 different places outside where you can mix sand, such as 4 grassy areas in a park or 4 different places on a driveway.
- 4 small containers, such as small paper cups or **upcycled** (reused) plastic yogurt containers
- Water
- Measuring cups

THE STEPS

1. Scoop 1 cup of sand onto each of your 4 locations.

2. Add ¼ cup of water to the sand in the first location, ⅓ cup of water to the second, ½ cup of water to the third, and 1 cup of water to the fourth.

3. Use your hands to mix the water with the sand in each location.

4. Fill one small container with sand from the first place. Pack the sand in tight. Turn the container upside down. Lift the container off.

5. Repeat with sand from the other 3 places. Which sandcastle sticks together the longest?

HOWS & WHYS: Water is a sticky material. Water sticks to itself. Water also sticks to other materials, including sand. The right amount of water will turn sand into a sticky, strong building material. Over time, the water will **evaporate**, and the sandcastle will crumble.

S T E A M Understanding water's stickiness involves the science of chemistry. When you create sandcastles, you are also making art.

Now Try This!: You can make permanent sandcastles by mixing 2 cups of sand with 1 cup of water and 1 cup of cornstarch. Have an adult mix everything together in an old pot and cook over low heat for about 5 minutes. Sculpt this mixture to make a castle. When it dries, it will be very hard.

TIDAL POWER

LEVEL OF DIFFICULTY: EASY
MESSY METER:
MEDIUM MESS
FROM BEGINNING TO END:
10 MINUTES
SEASONS:

MATERIALS

- Bucket with a handle
- Water

Gravity is the force that pulls objects together. Very large objects, like Earth and the moon, pull with the strongest force—strong enough to move the ocean and cause tides. In this experiment, you will create a force like gravity to see its effect on water. ***How do you think you could create a force like gravity?***

Hypothesis: ....

....

THE STEPS

1. Fill the bucket about ¼ full of water.

2. Turn the bucket upside down. What happens?

3. Refill the bucket about ¼ full of water again.

4. Grab the bucket by the handle and swing it hard in a big circle over your head. Does the water fall out of the bucket this time?

HOWS & WHYS: Ordinarily, if you turn a bucket upside down, gravity would cause the water to fall out. But when you swing a bucket over your head, you create something called **centripetal force**, which counteracts gravity and pushes the water back into the bucket. So, the water shouldn't fall out when you do this experiment, even when the bucket is upside down!

⬤ⓉⒺⒶⓂ **In this engineering modeling challenge, you applied the science of physics by exploring forces and motion.**

Now Try This!: In this experiment, you applied the centripetal force to the bucket while swinging it in a circle. Try modeling the centripetal force in other ways. For example, swing a ball on the end of a string and watch the centripetal force pull the string tight.

BEAR DEN

LEVEL OF DIFFICULTY: EASY

MESSY METER:

MEDIUM MESS

FROM BEGINNING TO END:

30 MINUTES

SEASONS:

MATERIALS

- Large piles of logs, sticks, branches, and dry leaves
- Mud (optional)
- 2 thermometers

? In winter, bears, turtles, hedgehogs, and other animals **hibernate**. These animals build a cozy den or nest, snuggle in, and enter a sleeplike state. In this experiment, you will engineer a den that would keep a bear warm for the winter. **Is it warmer inside or outside a den?**

Hypothesis: _____

THE STEPS

1. Find a spot outside to build your den. Look for an area out of the wind near a tree trunk or a large rock.

2. Use logs and sticks to frame a den that is large enough for you to fit inside.

3. Use branches and leaves to cover the frame so that wind can't get into your den. You can use mud to get the branches and leaves to stick to the frame—but be careful to keep the inside of your den dry.

4. Place one thermometer outside of your den, then go into your den with the other thermometer.

5. Spend 10 to 20 minutes playing in your den, then check both thermometers. Was it warmer inside your den than it was outside?

HOWS & WHYS: A den provides shelter from the wind and **insulation** from the cold. Air does not go in or out of the den. After you have been playing in the den, heat from your body warms up the air that is trapped in the den. Hibernating animals warm up their dens as they sleep.

S T E A M In this mechanical engineering challenge, you applied the science of physics by learning how to trap heat in an insulated space. When you built your den, you also practiced the art of architecture.

Now Try This!: For an advanced challenge, try building an outdoor shelter that would protect you overnight. Use a tarp to create a waterproof roof. Ask an adult to help you set up a sleeping pad and sleeping bag. When you go outside at night, make sure an adult knows where you are or comes with you.

WACKY WATERSHED

LEVEL OF DIFFICULTY: EASY

MESSY METER:

MEDIUM MESS

FROM BEGINNING TO END:

20 MINUTES

SEASONS:

? In this experiment, you will explore the flow of water over land by building a miniature **watershed**, an area of land that drains rainwater into a river or ocean (see diagram on page 81). **Where do you predict the water will flow?**

Hypothesis: _____

MATERIALS

- Garden, sandbox, or other outdoor area where you can dig and build with sand or soil
- Digging tool, like a shovel or hoe
- Water in a bucket or from a garden hose

THE STEPS

1. In a garden, sandbox, or other outdoor area, dig into the sand or soil to make a tiny **valley**, a low area between hills or mountains.

2. Use the material you dig to build up tiny mountains on both sides of your valley.

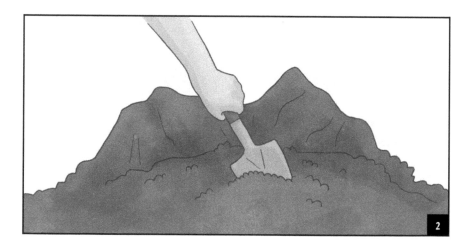

3. Continue digging and building until you have a miniature watershed with high- and lowland areas.

4. Pour water over your watershed, beginning at the top of a mountain. Watch where the water goes.

5. Keep pouring water over your watershed until it flows off and away. Follow the water as far as you can go. Does it flow into a storm drain, drainage ditch, or somewhere else?

HOWS & WHYS: Water flows over and above Earth's surface in a pattern called the **water cycle**. Rain falls from clouds onto watersheds. Rivers and streams flow into lakes and oceans. Water leaves Earth's surface when heat causes evaporation. Evaporated water condenses into clouds, and when the water drops in clouds are heavy enough, they fall back to Earth as rain. The water that is on Earth now is the same water that has been here for billions of years. The water you drink could have been sipped by a stegosaurus!

⑤①⑤④⑩ In this mechanical engineering experiment, you applied geological science and the art of sculpture.

Now Try This!: To explore how pollution impacts watersheds, add a small pile of brightly colored powdered drink mix to your miniature watershed. Observe when and where the water becomes polluted with the drink mix.

TERRIFIC TERRACES

LEVEL OF DIFFICULTY:
MEDIUM
MESSY METER:
MEDIUM MESS
FROM BEGINNING TO END:
30 MINUTES
SEASONS:

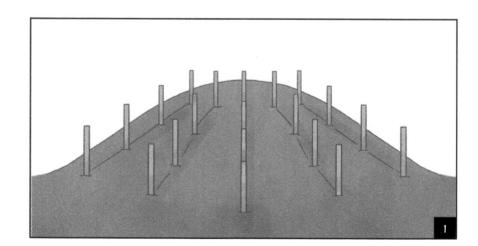

On many farms, a major problem is soil **erosion**: when rain and wind push soil off the land and into rivers, removing valuable nutrients and polluting waterways with dirt. **How can farmers plant their crops to prevent erosion?**

Hypothesis: ....
....

MATERIALS

- Garden or outdoor area with soil where you can dig and build
- Digging tool, like a shovel or hoe
- 20 sticks
- 12 to 20 medium-size stones or rocks
- Water

THE STEPS

1. In a garden or other outdoor area, use your digging tool to loosen the soil. Push the soil into a hill. Press 5 rows of 4 sticks into the soil in a row going down the hill to represent farm plants.

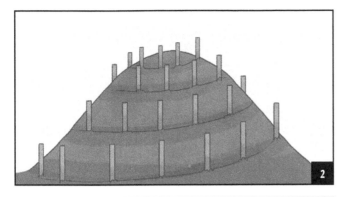

2. Build another soil hill. Press 20 sticks into the soil in a row going across the hill.

3. Build another soil hill. Pack the soil on one side of the hill into 3 big steps. These steps are **terraces**. Use stones or rocks to make the walls between the terraces strong. Press 4 sticks into 1 of the terraces.

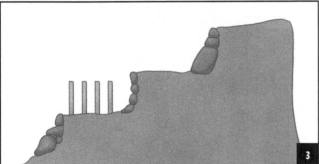

4. Pour water over each of your hills. Where did you see the most erosion? The least?

HOWS & WHYS: When farmers dig and plant soil in rows going across hills, the plants and their roots stop the flow of rainwater and the push of wind. This prevents erosion. Terraces also make the flow of rainwater pause because the soil on each terrace is flat.

S T E A M In this environmental engineering experiment, you applied agricultural technologies and geological science to solve a problem.

Now Try This!: Now that you have created model farms, plant seeds where you have placed your sticks. Bush bean seeds are a great choice for your model farm. Over time, the plants that grow from your seeds might stop erosion!

WHICH WEATHER?

LEVEL OF DIFFICULTY:
MEDIUM

MESSY METER: MINOR MESS

FROM BEGINNING TO END:
10 MINUTES TO SET UP,
FOLLOWED BY
DAILY CHECKS FOR
2 TO 3 WEEKS

SEASONS:

MATERIALS

- Scissors
- Balloon
- Glass jar
- 1 rubber band
- Tape
- 1 (5- to 8-inch) lightweight stick

? A **barometer** measures **air pressure**, the weight of air molecules pushing down on Earth. Air pressure is different on rainy days and sunny days. In this experiment, you will engineer a barometer and make observations to find the answer to the question: ***Do rainy days have high air pressure or low air pressure?***

Hypothesis: ....

....

THE STEPS

1. Use the scissors to cut the neck off a balloon.

2. Ask an adult to help you stretch the neckless balloon over the opening of a glass jar.

3. Secure the balloon on to the jar with a rubber band around the rim.

4. Tape a lightweight stick to the balloon so that it sticks out to the side.

5. Find a sheltered place outdoors where you can place your barometer.

6. Come back and check your barometer daily. When it's raining, does the stick tilt up or down?

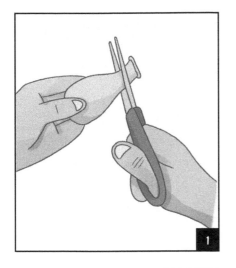

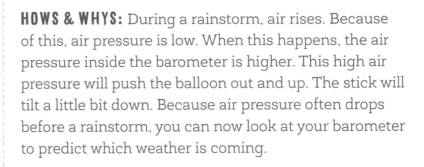

HOWS & WHYS: During a rainstorm, air rises. Because of this, air pressure is low. When this happens, the air pressure inside the barometer is higher. This high air pressure will push the balloon out and up. The stick will tilt a little bit down. Because air pressure often drops before a rainstorm, you can now look at your barometer to predict which weather is coming.

S T E A M In this mechanical engineering experiment, you applied the science of weather to build a piece of technology.

Now Try This!: Using paper and markers, create artwork to hang up behind your barometer. When the barometer points down, rainy weather is expected. Draw or paint a rainy scene at the bottom of your paper. High air pressure predicts clear skies. Create a sunny scene for the top of your paper.

BIOMIMICRY BRAINSTORM

LEVEL OF DIFFICULTY: HARD
MESSY METER: MINOR MESS
FROM BEGINNING TO END:
1 TO 2 HOURS
SEASONS:

MATERIALS

- A burr, prickly seed, or sticker seed
- 1 (2-inch) strip of Velcro
- Magnifying glass or hand lens (optional)
- Pencil
- Paper

? The outdoors gives engineers inspiration. In this challenge, you will observe a classic example of **biomimicry**, in which engineers develop products that imitate nature. Think of a problem in everyday life. **What would nature do to solve this problem?**

Hypothesis: _____

THE STEPS

1. Explore outside to find a burr, prickly seed, or sticker seed. Look for medium-size green plants growing in the sun or shade with round seeds that have rough edges. Burrs are easiest to find in late summer and fall.

2. Examine both sides of the piece of Velcro up close, using a magnifying glass if possible. How do the two sides of Velcro attach?

3. Think about problems in your everyday life. Do your shoes come untied? Are your backpack straps uncomfortable? Does the salt in your salt shaker stick together in a big clump?

4. On a piece of paper, draw a T-chart. On one side, write "problems" and on the other side, write "nature's solutions." For example, plants deal with the problem of dry surface soil by growing roots deep into wetter soil.

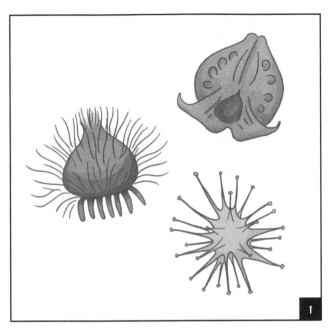

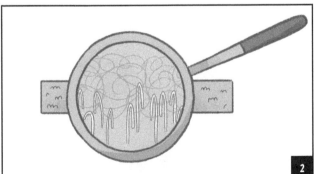

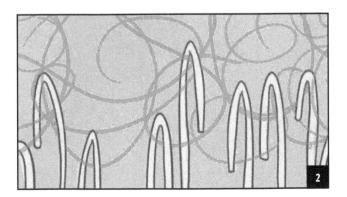

5. List 3 to 5 problems on the "problems" side of your T-chart.

6. Go outside and investigate nature. Look for nature's solutions to your problems. When you find one, add it to your T-chart with words or drawings.

7. Once you have found three possible solutions, choose one to try. Create the solution and see if it solves your problem.

8. Did your biomimicry brainstorming reveal helpful solutions?

HOWS & WHYS: The Swiss engineer George de Mestral invented Velcro after studying the burr seeds of a burdock plant. The shape of airplane wings was inspired by bird wings. Sticky gecko feet have inspired glue recipes, and solar panel designs have been inspired by tree leaves. A T-chart is a tool to support the brainstorming, or **ideation**, step of the engineering design process. Bio-mimicry brainstorming has led to some truly great engineering breakthroughs and is taught in engineering schools.

CONTINUED

(S)(T)(E)(A)(M) **When you completed the biomimicry brainstorming process, you were set to engineer a technology tool. Because observation is part of this process, you also used science.**

Now Try This!: Make a nature journal where you can draw and describe inspirations. For 1 to 2 weeks, go outside at different times of the day. Look at living things that are on land, underwater, and in the air. Explore, observe, and write in your journal. Create T-charts as you capture the solutions you brainstorm.

BERNOULLI'S BUBBLES

LEVEL OF DIFFICULTY: HARD

MESSY METER:

MEDIUM MESS

FROM BEGINNING TO END:

1 HOUR

SEASONS:

MATERIALS

- Bucket
- 6 cups water
- 1 cup dish soap
- ¼ cup corn syrup
- Bubble wand or homemade wand

 According to Bernoulli's principle, the faster air moves, the less pressure it has. Airplane engineers apply Bernoulli's principle to design planes that can fly. In this experiment, you will apply Bernoulli's principle to lift bubbles and keep them off the ground. **How long do you think you can keep a bubble in the air?**

Hypothesis: _____

Caution: Goggles will protect your eyes from bubble splashes.

THE STEPS

1. In a bucket, mix 6 cups of water, 1 cup of dish soap, and ¼ cup of corn syrup.

2. Dip a bubble wand into the bubble mixture. You can make your own bubble wand out of stems or vines by bending the stem into a loop that you can dip in the bubble mixture.

3. Blow bubbles!

4. Count how many seconds it takes the bubbles to fall to the ground.

5. Remember Bernoulli's principle: fast-moving air pushes with less pressure than slower-moving air. How could you

CONTINUED

create fast-moving air above a bubble or slower-moving air below a bubble? Try placing a fan nearby or blowing out air from your mouth near the bubbles.

6. Try at least 3 different strategies for keeping your bubble in the air.

7. Be sure to count how many seconds it takes your bubbles to fall to the ground while using each strategy.

HOWS & WHYS: Fast-moving air doesn't press down on bubbles as hard as slow-moving air. When you make the air above a bubble move faster or make the air below a bubble slow down, you are creating a force pushing up that scientists call **lift**. In cold weather, your bubbles might fly quite high. The heat from your breath causes bubbles to rise in cold air.

🅢 🅣 🅔 🅐 🅜 You used the science of aerodynamics to keep your bubbles in the air. Counting the number of seconds that the bubbles stayed in the air also involved math.

Now Try This!: To add a chemical engineering challenge to this experiment, change the bubble recipe. Cornstarch, baking powder, sugar, and honey are ingredients that might make your bubbles last longer.

SPOTLIGHT ON: WIND ENERGY ENGINEERS!

Wind energy engineers use the engineering design process to design wind farms, where many **wind turbines**, machines that capture wind energy, spin in the wind to make electricity. Wind farms make **sustainable energy** that powers our homes and businesses. What's wonderful about wind energy is that it does not make the greenhouse gases that lead to climate change.

Wind engineers need to understand the mechanical, electrical, and environmental engineering involved, as well as the way that wind moves through the place where the wind farm will be built. If you liked building structures or learning about Bernoulli's principle, consider becoming a wind energy engineer.

Chapter Five

ART

The outdoors can give never-ending inspiration for artists. In this chapter, you will use art to study nature, as well as use nature to inspire your art.

Art can be very useful during outdoor science experiments. In following experiments, you will use art skills to create a dummy butterfly to lure real butterflies to a special mud puddle. You will also create music with natural materials to learn about how bugs make sound.

Art can teach you about the outdoors. Taking impressions of leaves will show you how trees move. Making sun prints will help you understand how light can make chemical reactions occur. Studying rainbows and the colors of leaves will teach you the physics of light and color.

Letting the outdoors inspire your art can connect you with nature. Balancing rocks, making large-scale art with outdoor materials, and growing moss gardens helps you get acquainted with the place where you live. Understanding the landforms and living things around you will not only make you a more knowledgeable scientist, it will also make your home more special to you.

LASTING LEAVES

LEVEL OF DIFFICULTY: EASY

MESSY METER: MINOR MESS

FROM BEGINNING TO END:
20 MINUTES TO GATHER
AND PRESS LEAVES,
PLUS 10 MINUTES
1 WEEK LATER

SEASONS:

? **Botanists,** or plant scientists, collect plants in the wild and preserve them in **herbaria**, collections of dried plants glued to paper on which the botanist has made scientific notes. In this experiment, you will test the question: ***Is it easier to build an herbarium with pressed plants or plants that have dried naturally?***

Hypothesis: ....

....

MATERIALS

- ➔ Fresh green plants or leaves from outside
- ➔ 4 heavy books
- ➔ 6 full sheets of newspaper or paper towels
- ➔ 9 pieces of plain printer paper
- ➔ Glue

THE STEPS

1. Go outdoors and collect 2 of each kind of plant or leaf. For example, if you find a maple leaf and a dandelion, collect 2 maple leaves and 2 dandelions. Check with an adult first to make sure that it's okay to dig up the plant or pull off the leaves.

2. Set 1 of each kind of plant or leave aside to dry naturally.

3. Press the remaining plants and leaves. To do this, layer your materials from bottom to top by putting;

   - 1 closed book on the bottom
   - 1 full sheet of newspaper (folded twice) on top of the book
   - 1 piece of plain paper on top of the newspaper
   - 1 plant or leaf on top of the plain paper

- Another piece of plain paper on top of the plant or leaf
- Another full sheet of newspaper (folded twice) on top of the plain paper
- Another heavy book on the top

4. Repeat until you have pressed 1 of each kind of plant or leaf.

5. Wait 1 week for all of your plants and leaves to dry.

6. When the plants and leaves are dry, glue them onto plain paper. On the paper, write the name of the plant if you know it, along with where you collected it and the date. Which plants and leaves were the easiest to work with?

CONTINUED

HOWS & WHYS: When you pressed your plants and leaves, the plain paper kept them clean. The newspaper absorbed all of the water, and the books made everything flat. Clean, flat, dry specimens are perfect for herbaria because they show what the plants look like in real life while fitting into a flat book that botanists can carry easily when they are exploring outdoors.

⬤S ⬤T ⬤E ⬤A ⬤M **While creating a work of botanical art, you applied the scientific method to discover the best way to preserve plants for an herbarium.**

Now Try This!: You can create a whole book of pressed plants. Keep collecting, pressing, and gluing plants and leaves until you have large collection. Keep the pages in a neat stack in a folder or glue them into a blank book.

MUD PUDDLING

LEVEL OF DIFFICULTY: EASY

MESSY METER:

MEDIUM MESS

FROM BEGINNING TO END:

20 MINUTES

SEASON:

MATERIALS

- ➲ Paper or flowers
- ➲ Colored markers
- ➲ Sunny dirt patch
- ➲ Water
- ➲ Salt

? Observing animals, including insects, is a super fun part of outdoor science. But it can be hard to find them! In this experiment, you will lure butterflies to a mud puddle and observe their activities. **Why do butter-flies love mud puddles?**

Hypothesis: ....

THE STEPS

1. Make a dummy butterfly. You can do this one of three ways: draw a butterfly on paper and cut it out, put flowers together in the shape of a butterfly, or fold an origami butterfly.

2. Find a sunny dirt patch outside.

CONTINUED

3. Add water and a sprinkling of salt to the dirt to make a salty mud puddle.

4. Place your dummy butterfly at the edge of the mud puddle.

5. Hide quietly and wait for butterflies to come. They might not come right away—it's okay for you to go away and check back later. When the butterflies do come, watch closely to see what they are doing.

HOWS & WHYS: Dummy butterflies attract real butterflies because butterflies like to be in groups. Scientists, who call a group of butterflies a **kaleidoscope**, **swarm**, or **flutter**, believe that being in a group protects butterflies from predators. Mud might not be very appetizing for you or me, but butterflies think it's delicious. Butterflies need to eat the salt in mud, so you might see them drinking from mud puddles.

S T E A M In this artistic experiment, you used **entomology**, the science of insects, and your dummy butterfly was a technology tool.

Now Try This!: Monarch butterflies are an **endangered** species. You can help monarchs and other butterflies by planting butterfly-feeding flowers like milkweed, coneflower, and phlox.

SUN PRINTS

LEVEL OF DIFFICULTY:
MEDIUM
MESSY METER: MINOR MESS
FROM BEGINNING TO END:
10 MINUTES TO SET
UP, 2 MINUTES (IF
USING SUNPRINT
PAPER) OR 3 HOURS (IF
USING CONSTRUCTION
PAPER) TO WAIT, AND
10 MINUTES TO FINISH
SEASONS:

MATERIALS

- 5 to 10 leaves, flowers, stones, and other outdoor found objects
- 2 or 3 pieces of Sunprint paper (available in art stores) or dark construction paper
- Plastic wrap (optional)

 Sunscreen protects skin from **ultraviolet** sun rays. The damaging effects of ultraviolet sunshine can be seen on **photosensitive** (light-sensitive) materials, including Sunprint paper and construction paper. In this experiment, you will create a design using outdoor objects on photosensitive paper. ***How will the paper change in the sunlight?***

Hypothesis: _____

_____

⚠ Caution: Never look directly at the sun.

THE STEPS

1. On a very sunny day, go outside and gather 5 to 10 objects with interesting shapes, like leaves with jagged edges, flowers, and a variety of stones.

2. In a strong sunbeam, lay a piece of Sunprint paper or dark construction paper on the ground.

3. Arrange your found objects in an interesting pattern. If you are using Sunprint paper, work quickly!

4. If your objects are light, place a layer of plastic wrap over your work so nothing flies away.

5. Leave your design for 2 to 4 minutes for Sunprint paper or 2 to 3 hours for construction paper.

CONTINUED

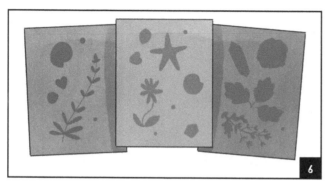

6. Remove the objects. The paper under the objects will be unchanged. The rest of the paper was changed by sunlight. How did it change?

HOWS & WHYS: Sunprint paper is covered with dark photosensitive chemicals. When ultraviolet light hits the chemicals in Sunprint paper, they turn into different chemicals. The new chemicals don't have the same color and the paper looks lighter. Construction paper is made with dyes that also lose their color when they are in sunlight.

S T E A M You explored the science of **photochemistry**, the study of chemical reactions that involve light. Photochemistry is important to understanding plants and solar energy.

Now Try This!: For an advanced science experiment, compare the effects of sunlight on different colors of construction paper. Set the same found objects in the same pattern on sheets of different colors of construction paper and notice how the different colors change.

TRUE COLORS

LEVEL OF DIFFICULTY: EASY

MESSY METER: MINOR MESS

FROM BEGINNING TO END:
20 MINUTES

SEASON:

If you live in a place that doesn't have fall, you can still go on a color-gathering hike to collect leaves of as many colors as possible.

MATERIALS

- A bunch of leaves gathered outdoors
- Magnifying glass or hand lens (optional)

? Most leaves are green because of a special chemical called **chlorophyll**. Chlorophyll is a green chemical that can **absorb** light and turn it into energy that plants use in photosynthesis, a process in which they convert energy from sunlight into energy for food. In the fall, leaves turn colors. In this experiment, you will gather a rainbow of leaves and explore the question: **Why do leaves change colors in the fall?**

Hypothesis: ....

....

THE STEPS

1. Explore outdoors, searching for as many different colors of leaves as you can find. Search for red, orange, yellow, brown, purple, and silver leaves. Gather a few green leaves, too.

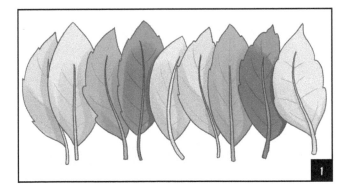

CONTINUED

2. Look closely at the colorful leaves. How are they different from the green leaves?

3. Touch the colorful leaves and the green leaves. Notice their texture.

4. Smell the leaves. How are the colorful leaves different from the green leaves?

5. Use your observations to make another hypothesis: Do the colorful leaves photosynthesize the way that the green leaves do?

HOWS & WHYS: For most plants, photosynthesis can't happen in the fall or winter months. When the days get shorter and temperatures get colder, chlorophyll breaks down and disappears from the leaves. The fall colors that you see were there in the leaves all summer long. Now that the chlorophyll is gone, these bright colors shine through.

S T E A M Exploring colors strengthens your art skills. Observing is a science skill. Comparing is a math skill.

Now Try This!: The colors you find in nature can be used to **dye**, or give color to, fabric. Soak some white fabric for 1 hour in a mixture of ½ cup of salt and 8 cups of water. In an old pot, have an adult help you boil the fabric in water for about 45 minutes with about 2 cups of leaves, berries, or roots. Rinse in cold water and air-dry.

TREE SECRETS

LEVEL OF DIFFICULTY: EASY

MESSY METER: MINOR MESS

FROM BEGINNING TO END:
30 MINUTES

SEASONS:

Trees may look like they are holding still, but underneath their bark, they are always pumping water up from the ground and sugars down from their leaves. The tubes that trees use to pump materials can been seen in the **venation**, or tube patterns, on their leaves. In this experiment, you will use crayons, paper, and trees to create rubbings that reveal leaf venation. **What patterns will you find?**

Hypothesis: ....

....

MATERIALS

- 3 different leaves from outside
- 4 sheets of paper
- Sidewalk or a large, flat rock
- 1 or more crayons

THE STEPS

1. Go outside and gather 3 different leaves. Find leaves with different shapes, sizes, and textures.

2. Sandwich a leaf between 2 pieces of paper and set it down on a sidewalk or large, flat rock.

3. Peel the paper label off a crayon and rub the crayon over the top sheet of paper. The shape of the leaf should soon appear.

4. Reusing the bottom paper, repeat steps 2 and 3 with 2 more leaves.

5. What pattern did you notice?

CONTINUED

HOWS & WHYS: Plants have to move sugar from the tips of their leaves all the way down to their roots—and they have to move water in the opposite direction! Leaf veins are little tubes that stretch from leaves to stems, and from stems to central tubes inside tree trunks. To move sugar in and water out, all leaves have veins that start at the center and reach outward, like the rays of the sun or the petals of a flower.

S T E A M In addition to practicing the scientific skill of observation, you also applied the science of botany.

Now Try This!: Did you know that you can make bark rubbings? Just place a piece of paper on the outside of a tree and rub your crayon back and forth. Try doing a bark rubbing on half of a piece of paper, with a leaf rubbing from the same tree on the other half.

RAINBOW REFRACTIONS

LEVEL OF DIFFICULTY: EASY

MESSY METER:

MEDIUM MESS

FROM BEGINNING TO END:

20 MINUTES

SEASONS:

MATERIALS

→ Garden hose with spray nozzle

 After a rainstorm, you might be lucky enough to see a rainbow. Rainbows appear when the sun shines after it rains. Sunbeams bounce around inside the raindrops and separate into the colors of the rainbow. In this experiment, you will discover the answer to the question: **Where should you stand to see a rainbow?**

Hypothesis: ....

....

Caution: Never look directly at the sun.

THE STEPS

1. Find a sunny area that you can reach with the garden hose.

2. Set the spray nozzle to a mist or gentle spray.

3. Turn the water on.

4. Stand in different places until you see a rainbow.

CONTINUED

3

HOWS & WHYS: When light shines through two different materials, like water and air, **refraction**, or bending of light, happens. In this experiment, the white sunlight refracted into many different colors. You can only see the rainbow if the sun is behind you and the light refracts toward you, as shown in the diagram below.

⑧①⑤④Ⓜ **Exploring light refraction involves the science of physics.**

Now Try This!: Make another rainbow and notice the order of colors. You should see red on one end and violet on the other. The next color after red will be orange, then yellow, green, blue, indigo, and violet. Rainbow colors always appear in this order because of the **wavelengths** of the colors of light. Scientists call this order of colors ROY G. BIV for short.

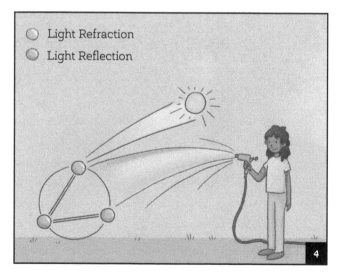

◯ Light Refraction
◯ Light Reflection

4

ROCK BALANCING

LEVEL OF DIFFICULTY:
MEDIUM

MESSY METER: MINOR MESS

FROM BEGINNING TO END:
30 MINUTES

SEASONS:

MATERIALS

- 3 or 4 large rocks (about the size of two fists each)

 Rocks and stones can be used to create wonderful outdoor art in all seasons. Cairns are sturdy stacks of rocks used to mark trails or just to make a place more beautiful. In this experiment, you will explore the science of physics to create a rock-balancing sculpture. **What is the secret to getting round rocks to balance in a stack?**

Hypothesis: ....

....

Caution: Be sure to wear closed-toed shoes to protect your feet from falling rocks.

THE STEPS

Go outside and collect a variety of rocks for your sculpture.

1. Find a rock with a dip and set it on the ground with the dip facing up. The dip will make a good spot for setting a second rock on top of the first rock.

2. Pick up a second rock and work to balance it on top of the first rock. You may need to try several different ways to get this to work.

3. If you are feeling frustrated, find another rock with a bigger hollow on top or a rougher texture to use as the base of your sculpture.

CONTINUED

4. How sturdy is the ground under your bottom rock? If you wiggle your bottom rock into a pile of gravel, sand, or dirt, it will be steadier.

5. Once you have one rock balanced on top of another, it's time to add a third rock. Remember that you may need to try many times before you get your rocks to balance.

6. How high can you make your rock sculpture?

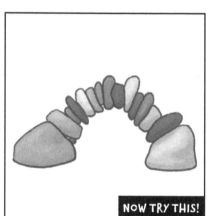

HOWS & WHYS: Rocks will balance when they touch at 3 different contact points. These 3 points form a sturdy triangle that will hold weight. The contact points must stay connected. **Friction**, or resistance to movement between the rocks, is highest when the rocks have rough textures. Friction helps keep the contact points connected. Eventually, gravity will pull the rocks apart.

S T E A M The art of rock balancing involves the science of physics as well as geometry (math).

Now Try This!: For an advanced challenge, paint the rocks different colors before you stack them, and create a rock arch. Invite a friend, sibling, or adult to help hold the rocks of the arch until you get the last rock in place. Once all of the rocks are in the arch, the friction between the rocks should hold the arch in place.

LAND ART

LEVEL OF DIFFICULTY:
MEDIUM

MESSY METER:
MEDIUM MESS

FROM BEGINNING TO END:
1 HOUR

SEASONS:

MATERIALS

❯ Leaves, rocks, flowers, branches, snow, or ice (whatever you find outdoors)

? Nature is full of beautiful shapes and colors. Land art uses patterns found outdoors to inspire all-natural sculptures. Some are so big they can be seen from space! In this experiment, you will explore, gather materials, and build your own land art. **What colors and patterns will you find to inspire your sculpture?**

Hypothesis: ....

....

THE STEPS

1. Choose an outdoor area and explore for 10 minutes. Search for interesting shapes (like the spiral of a snail's shell), colors (like red autumn leaves on green grass), and patterns (like shadows from tree branches on snow).

CONTINUED

2. Gather materials for a sculpture, like pebbles, acorns, flowers, and sticks. Try to find bright colors.

3. In the beautiful area, clear an area for your sculpture.

4. Set your materials down in the place and think about what you would like to make. Can you make the spiral of a snail's shell with red leaves on green grass, or arrange tall sticks to make shadows in the snow?

5. Big shapes and contrasting colors will make your land art easier to see. How big can you make your sculpture? Can you put something dark on something light?

6. Begin building your land art. Take your time and create something awesome.

7. Invite an adult to see your land art or take a photo to share.

8. Land art does not last forever. Enjoy your sculpture while it lasts and start dreaming of your next creation.

HOWS & WHYS: Land art deepens our understanding of landscapes and natural materials. Although these observations may not seem scientific at first, artistic ways of knowing add to our understanding of nature. For example, an advanced physics lab in Sweden used land art to make earth mounds that reduced disruptive traffic vibrations.

S T E A M Land art involves the art of sculpture and the scientific practice of making observations.

Now Try This!: Try making **earthworks**, art made by reshaping the land. Dig up tunnels, make soil mountains, and craft spiral shapes.

SEED MOSAICS

LEVEL OF DIFFICULTY: HARD

MESSY METER:
MEDIUM MESS

FROM BEGINNING TO END:
1½ HOURS

SEASONS:

MATERIALS

- Small handful of
  5 different kinds of seeds
  each (for example,
  acorns, sunflower seeds,
  and cottonwood seeds)
- 5 small containers (cups,
  bowls, or storage
  containers)
- 1 piece of card stock,
  paper plate, or flattened
  cereal box
- All-purpose white glue

? The ancient craft of seed art involves creating mosaics, or pictures made from many small things, out of seeds. In this experiment, you will gather and sort seeds for your own seed art. As you do so, you will discover: **How can seeds be scientifically sorted?**

Hypothesis: _____

THE STEPS

1. Go outside and gather 5 or more kinds of seeds. Try to collect a small handful of each type of seed. In winter, you can use beans, corn, lentils, and other seeds from your kitchen pantry or spice rack.

2. Organize your seeds so that you have one kind of seed in each of your containers. As you organize, decide on a scientific method for sorting the seeds. Would it be better to sort by type, size, texture, color, or shape?

3. Draw a picture on your card stock, paper plate, or cereal box cardboard. Large, simple shapes are best to start.

4. Trace over the edges of your picture with glue.

5. Place seeds on top of the glue.

6. Continue adding seeds to your drawing.

CONTINUED

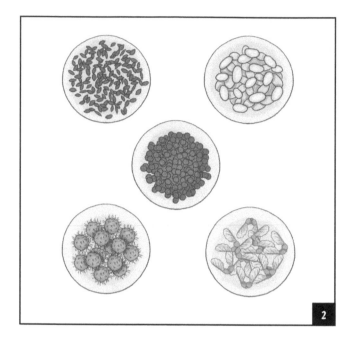

7. Once you have finished the lines, fill in the centers of your shapes.

8. Notice how using different seeds can give your seed art interesting colors and textures.

HOWS & WHYS: When scientists sort seeds, size, shape, texture, and color are all important factors. Some seeds, like maple samaras, also called helicopter seeds, are so special that you can recognize them just by looking at them. Seed art gives people opportunities to look at and get to know different kinds of seeds.

S T E A M Because you sorted seeds, math was involved in this art-based experiment.

Now Try This!: Crop art is a kind of art that only uses seeds from farms and gardens. Many county and state fairs have crop art competitions. Find the nearest crop art competition and enter your best seed art.

GATHERING MOSS

LEVEL OF DIFFICULTY: HARD

MESSY METER:
MEDIUM MESS

FROM BEGINNING TO END:
1 HOUR TO SET UP, PLUS
5 MINUTES EVERY DAY
FOR SEVERAL WEEKS

SEASON:

MATERIALS

- 2 cups moss from outdoors
- 1 magnifying glass or hand lens (optional)
- 2 cups buttermilk
- 1 old blender
- 3 large objects with hard, flat surfaces such as stones, flowerpot saucers, logs, or bark
- Paintbrush

Moss is a short, soft, springy plant that comes in many shades of green. In this experiment, you will make a moss mixture that you can paint on outdoor surfaces to grow your own moss garden. **Where will moss grow best?**

Hypothesis: _____

Caution: Adult supervision is needed while working with a blender. Do not drink the moss mixture. Be sure to clean your blender thoroughly after this experiment.

THE STEPS

1. Hunt for moss outdoors. Moss loves water, so look for shady spots near lakes, rivers, ponds, and streams.

2. Gather about 2 cups of moss. Be careful not to take all of the moss that you find. Leave enough so that it can grow back.

3. You can use more than one type of moss. A mix of mosses works best!

4. Bring your moss home.

CONTINUED

5. Study your moss up close, using your magnifying lens if you have one. What do you notice about the shape of a moss plant?

6. Wash the moss gently to remove stones, stick, and bugs.

7. Combine 2 cups of moss and 2 cups of buttermilk in an old blender.

8. Blend the moss and the buttermilk together to make a thick moss milkshake.

9. Place 3 large objects with hard, flat surfaces, like stones, flowerpot saucers, logs, or bark in 3 different places outside. One place should be in the sun, one place should be in the shade, and one place should have some sun and some shade.

10. Use a paintbrush to paint a thick layer of your moss milkshake on top of each object. You can create patterns as you paint. Use up all of the milkshake.

11. To grow, your moss needs to stay moist (not soaking wet). Water it gently every day for 1 to 2 months.

12. Which place was best for growing moss?

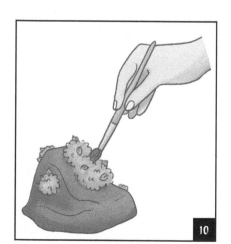

HOWS & WHYS: Buttermilk has several ingredients that help moss grow: sugar for food, protein to keep germs away, and acid—moss loves acid. Unlike other plants, moss has no tubes inside to move water from the ground up. Instead, moss has to absorb water, so it needs to stay moist. Moss usually doesn't grow in sunny places because sunlight dries the moss.

S T E A M Your art-based moss experiment involved botany, the science of plants, as well as blender technology and engineering skills used in horticulture, the art of gardening.

Now Try This!: For an advanced botany challenge, separate a single moss plant. Study it using your magnifying lens. Can you find the rootlike **rhizoid** that anchors the moss? Can you find the green part of the moss where **photosynthesis** happens?

MUSICAL BUGS

LEVEL OF DIFFICULTY: HARD

MESSY METER: MINOR MESS

FROM BEGINNING TO END:
30 MINUTES

SEASONS:

MATERIALS

- A few sticks, rocks, and stones
- Tree with rough bark

? Bugs buzz, vibrate, tap, pop, and even whistle. The most common bug music is stridulation, where bugs rub their legs or wings together. Bug music can defend against predators, warn others of danger, or help bugs find one another. In this experiment, you will build your own bug instrument to join in the bug music of your neighborhood.

Hypothesis: ....

....

THE STEPS

1. In late summer or early fall, go outside on a warm evening.

2. Explore until you hear insects chirping.

3. Listen closely to the sound. This is made by insects rubbing their legs or wings together.

4. Can you find the insects that are stridulating? The most common stridulating insects are grasshoppers, but beetles and other bugs stridulate, too.

5. Find a variety of sticks, rocks, and stones and bring them to a tree with rough bark.

6. Try dragging a stick or rock gently across the tree bark. Does this make a sound?

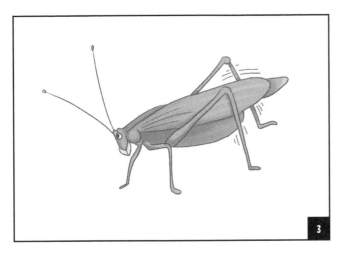

3

7. Experiment with your materials until you can make a sound like the bugs around you. Making a musical instrument can be very challenging. Keep trying different combinations.

8. Would it be easier to make bug music with your voice? See if you can imitate the sounds you hear with your voice.

9. Once you have made a stridulation sound, listen to see if any bugs respond.

HOWS & WHYS: Insects have special ridges on their legs and wings to help them make music. In crickets, the left and right wings have different bumpy parts that drag across each other whenever the wings connect. The number and size of the bumps, along with the way the cricket moves its wings, make each song special. While the ridges in tree bark can model these shapes, nothing can truly stridulate except an insect.

S T E A M In this entomology, or bug science, experiment, you applied the science of music. Because you had to try and try again, engineering design was also involved.

Now Try This!: Now that you know more about how stridulation works, try engineering an insect instrument using a combination of household materials (like cardboard tubes, rubber bands, and paper) and outdoor materials (like sticks, leaves, and pebbles).

SPOTLIGHT ON: CARTOGRAPHERS!

Cartographers are mapmakers. To make great maps, cartographers make detailed observations, do careful research, and take the time to create artistic and accurate drawings of the world's landforms and cities.

Cartography involves science, technology, math, and art. The science of **geology**, or earth science, is how cartographers study the landforms they will draw. Mapmakers use many advanced technologies, including **satellites**, machines that have been launched into space and float above Earth. Cartographers use math to find the **scale**, or distance relationships, for each map.

The art of cartography involves using color, labels, and design to make maps easy for people to read and understand. Many maps are so beautiful that people display them as art in their homes, schools, and businesses. If you enjoy sharing your scientific observations through art, cartography might be the career for you!

Chapter Six

MATH

Math is everywhere outdoors, from the number of petals on a flower to the spiral of a snail's shell. Math can show how objects in nature are the same or different. STEAM professionals who work outdoors use math every day, and in this chapter, you can, too!

Scientists like you can use math to understand nature. Many of nature's great forces, including the force of gravity (which pulls objects down to Earth) can be best explained using math. Geometry, the math of shapes and angles, can be used to describe and measure objects and nature and their movement. Math helps scientists collect and understand **data**, or scientific information.

In this chapter, you will use math to compare, measure, and count snowflakes, puddles, pine cones, and more. Your data will include the speed of wind, the height of trees, and the shapes of the paths of flying objects. As you work, you will sharpen your math skills, becoming a more and more capable scientist.

While doing the experiments in this chapter, you may want to write down some of your data and calculations. Go for it! The more you write, think, and imagine numbers, the more you will be able to do with math.

PINE CONE PETALS

MATERIALS

- ➲ Ruler or tape measure
- ➲ 1 pine cone
- ➲ 1 container of water (big enough to hold the pine cone)

? Pine cones are seed holders for **coniferous**, or cone-bearing, trees and shrubs. The seeds are hidden deep down inside the pine cones. When pine cones get wet, they close up to protect the seeds. *How much smaller, in inches (or centimeters), will the width of a pine cone become when it is wet?*

Hypothesis: ....

....

THE STEPS

1. Use a ruler or tape measure to find the width of a pine cone in inches (or centimeters).

2. Place the pine cone in a container of water

3. Check the pine cone every minute for 10 minutes, or until it has closed up.

4. Take the pine cone out of the water and measure its width. How much smaller is it now?

5. Leave the pine cone to dry. In a few days, it will be back to its normal shape.

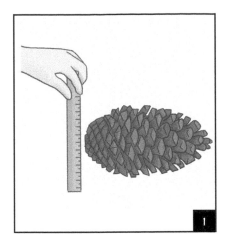

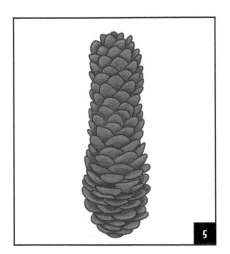

HOWS & WHYS: The bottom of each of the pine cone's **scales** (which look like petals) are **hydroscopic**, which means that the pine cone's scales absorb water, puff up, and close. This protects the seeds inside the pine cone, so that they stay dry and don't decay or get moldy in the rain.

⑤①⑤④Ⓜ In this math experiment, you measured and compared the width of a pine cone in wet and dry conditions. Because you collected this information to answer a scientific question, you did science.

Now Try This!: Try dunking a variety of pine cones into water to see how quickly they close up. Do some types of pine cones take longer to close, or to dry out and open again?

CATCH THE WIND

LEVEL OF DIFFICULTY:
MEDIUM

MESSY METER: MINOR MESS

FROM BEGINNING TO END:
30 MINUTES

SEASONS:

? Scientists use a tool called a windsock to measure the speed and direction of the wind. Windsocks are often used at airports. In this experiment, you will make a windsock using natural materials. *How will your windsock move when you catch the wind?*

Hypothesis: ....

MATERIALS

- 1 piece of paper (any color)
- Stapler, glue, or tape
- Hole punch
- 1 vine, 12 to 18 inches long
- 6 leaves on long stems
- Markers

THE STEPS

1. Roll the piece of paper into a tube and staple, glue, or tape the edges down.

2. Punch 2 holes at one end of the tube, across from each other.

3. Thread a vine through the holes and tie it to make a loop.

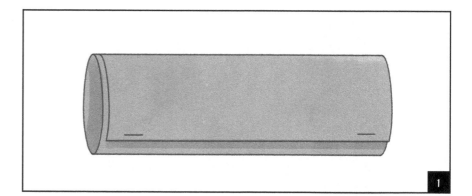

1

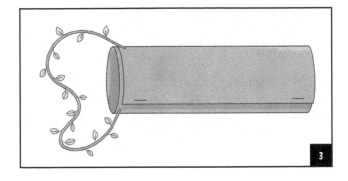

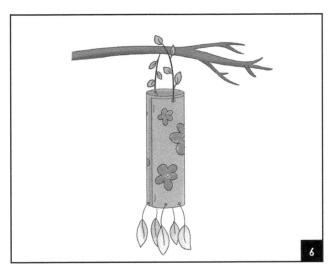

4. Punch 6 holes around the bottom of the tube. Thread the stems of leaves through the holes. Staple, glue, or tape the stems to the tube.

5. Use markers to decorate your windsock.

6. Hang your windsock outdoors where it can swing freely. Observe its position during calm and windy days. How does your windsock move in the wind?

HOWS & WHYS: When wind passes through a windsock, it lifts the windsock up. Mathematicians measure the position of a windsock to the ground using **angles**. When there is no wind, a windsock will hang toward the ground at a zero-degree angle. When the wind is strong, the windsock will lift 90 degrees to fly **parallel** to the ground.

S T E A M In addition to the science of weather, or **meteorology**, you used art in this math experiment.

Now Try This!: An **anemometer** is another kind of wind-measuring tool. To make your own anemometer, begin with a pinwheel. Use a marker to color one of the curls a bright color. Hold the pinwheel in the wind and count how many times the colorful curl spins past you in one minute.

JUST A PHASE

LEVEL OF DIFFICULTY: EASY

MESSY METER: MINOR MESS

FROM BEGINNING TO END:
5 MINUTES TO START,
FOLLOWED BY TWO
SHORT CHECK-INS 1 AND
2 HOURS LATER

SEASONS:

MATERIALS

➲ Cup of water

➲ Ruler or measuring tape

? After a rainstorm, the ground is covered with puddles. Eventually, the puddles dry up. In this experiment, you will observe the changes in **volume**, or space, that happen when a puddle seems to disappear. **How will the volume of a puddle change?**

Hypothesis: _____

_____

THE STEPS

1. Pour a cup of water on the ground outside. It's best to use a sidewalk or flat driveway so that the water does not sink down into the ground.

2. Use a ruler or measuring tape to measure the width of the puddle, from one side to another.

3. After 1 hour, measure the width of the puddle again. How has it changed?

4. After 1 more hour, measure the puddle a third time. Has it changed again?

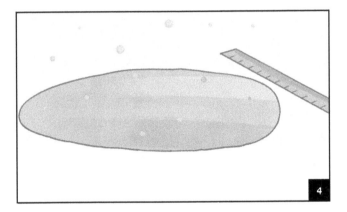

HOWS & WHYS: Water in a puddle slowly changes **phases**, from liquid to gas. This is called **evaporation**. One by one, tiny drops of water float away from the puddle and into the air. Although some water will sink into the ground, most of it evaporates into the air, where it will eventually condense as water in a cloud, then fall as rain. Evaporation causes the volume of the puddle to shrink. Because the width of a puddle is a part of its volume, you saw the width of the puddle shrink.

🅢 🅣 🅔 🅐 🅜 **You applied the science of chemistry when measuring evaporation in this experiment.**

Now Try This!: Temperature affects how quickly water evaporates. Try pouring a cup of water in a sunny spot and a cup of water in a shady spot. Does one of the puddles shrink faster? Hint: Be sure that both puddles are on the same kind of ground (sidewalk, grass, leaves, or dirt) because water sinks differently into different kinds of ground.

BUCKET FLOAT

LEVEL OF DIFFICULTY: EASY

MESSY METER: MINOR MESS

FROM BEGINNING TO END:
20 MINUTES

SEASONS:

MATERIALS

- As many outdoor materials as you can find, such as rocks, pine cones, feathers, leaves, sticks, vegetables, fruits, and flower petals
- Large bucket of water, or another place where objects can float on water, such as a pond or lake

 If you drop a pine cone in a river or stream, it will either float or sink. If you make a sailboat out of leaves and twigs, it might sail or it might sink. In this experiment, you will work with many different outdoor materials to explore the question: **What makes something float or sink?**

Hypothesis: ....

....

Caution: Make sure you have an adult with you, because you'll be working with water.

THE STEPS

1. Collect many different types of outdoor materials.

2. Carefully hold each item in your hand, noticing how heavy or light it feels.

3. Place the materials in a bucket of water and notice if each one floats or sinks.

4. What do the items that sink have in common?

5. What do the items that float have in common?

HOWS & WHYS: Density is a mathematical measurement of how much matter, or material, is packed into a certain amount of volume, or space. Materials that sink have a greater density than water. Very dense materials like stones almost always sink, but there are a few kinds of rocks that have air bubbles inside of them and can float. Materials that float have less density than water. Feathers usually float, but if they get really wet, they start to take up less volume and their density goes up—then they might sink!

S T E A M Working with density involves the sciences of chemistry and physics, and understanding density is important for engineers.

Now Try This!: Can you take a material that normally sinks and make it float? To do this, you can increase a dense item's volume by stretching it out or by connecting it to a floating object. For example, a large floating leaf can become a raft that helps a pebble float.

PROJECTILE PARABOLAS

LEVEL OF DIFFICULTY:
MEDIUM
MESSY METER: MINOR MESS
FROM BEGINNING TO END:
30 MINUTES
SEASONS:

MATERIALS

- 2 rubber bands
- Masking tape or duct tape
- 10 to 20 small, lightweight outdoor objects, like small pine cones, seeds, or berries

 In this experiment, you will build a simple slingshot and use it to launch projectiles, objects shot into the air. Gravity, the force that pulls objects to Earth, will bring your projectiles down to the ground. **What shape will the path of your projectiles make?**

Hypothesis: _____

Caution: Always shoot a slingshot away from people and animals.

THE STEPS

1. To build your slingshot, begin by overlapping 2 rubber bands.

2. Tie a knot in the rubber bands by holding the left edge of the right rubber band. Bring this edge under the right side of the left rubber band. Pull this edge to the right so that it folds over the right side of the left rubber band. Then pass this edge under the right edge of the right rubber band and pull it tight. The rubber band on the right is the handle for your slingshot.

3. Wrap tape around the rubber band on the left to make a scooped launchpad for your projectiles.

4. Go outside and collect a pile of 10 to 20 small, lightweight objects, like small pine cones, berries, or flowers.

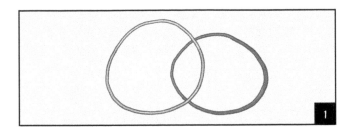

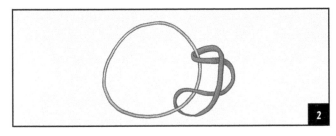

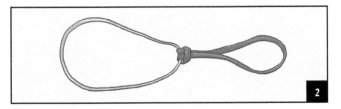

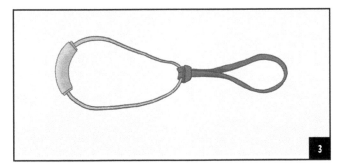

5. Place an object in the scooped launchpad of your slingshot.

6. Facing away from people and animals, pull the launchpad down and the handle up and to one side.

7. Release the launchpad to shoot your projectile up into the air. Watch the path of your projectile.

8. Repeat steps 5, 6, and 7 until you know the shape of the path that your projectiles made.

HOWS & WHYS: A projectile that is shot over Earth will be pulled back to the ground in a path that makes a shape called a parabola, a curved arc. At first, the projectile moves in the direction it is launched by the force of the slingshot. Later, the projectile moves in the direction it is pulled by Earth's gravity.

CONTINUED

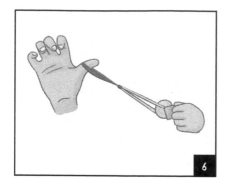

S T E A M In addition to studying geometry, the mathematics of shapes and angles, you also applied engineering skills by building your own slingshot.

Now Try This!: Use your engineering skills to modify and improve your slingshot. You could use larger rubber bands or more rubber bands. You could attach the rubber bands to a Y-shaped stick. Test your new slingshot to see if it can launch projectiles higher and farther.

TREETOP MATH

LEVEL OF DIFFICULTY:
MEDIUM
MESSY METER: MINOR MESS
FROM BEGINNING TO END:
45 MINUTES
SEASONS:

MATERIALS

- ➔ 1 stick, the same length as the distance from your outstretched hand to your eye
- ➔ 3 coniferous trees, such as pines, spruces, or firs
- ➔ 3 deciduous trees, such as maples, oaks, or birches
- ➔ Tape measure (10 feet or longer)

Trees come in all shapes and sizes. **Foresters**, or forest managers, need to know the height and **crown spread** (how far a tree's branches reach) of the trees in their forests. In this experiment, you will compare the height and crown spread of two different kinds of trees. **Will coniferous (evergreen) or deciduous (leaf-dropping) trees be taller and broader?**

Hypothesis: ....

THE STEPS

1. Hold your stick in one hand with your arm straight out from your body.

2. Stand looking at your first coniferous tree so that the tree appears to be the same height as the sick. You may need to walk toward or away from your tree to make this happen.

3. The height of the tree is equal to the distance from where you are standing to the base of the tree. Use the tape measure to measure this distance.

4. Record the height of this first tree, and repeat steps 2 and 3 for 2 more coniferous trees and 3 deciduous trees.

CONTINUED

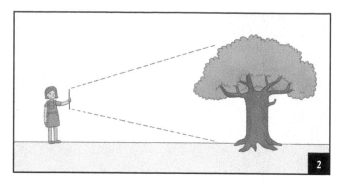

5. Add the heights of the 3 coniferous trees and divide this number by 3 to find the average coniferous tree height. Repeat for the 3 deciduous trees.

6. Return to the first coniferous tree. Stand under its branches and look up. At the ends of the branches where the leaves stop, mark the ground with a stick or pine cone. Go to the opposite side of the tree and find the ends of the branches where the leaves stop. Measure the distance from the opposite edges of the tree. This is the crown spread.

7. Repeat step 6 for the 2 remaining coniferous trees and all 3 deciduous trees.

8. Add the crown spreads of the 3 coniferous trees and divide this number by 3 to find the average coniferous crown spread.

9. Repeat for the deciduous trees.

10. According to the trees you studied, are coniferous trees or deciduous trees taller? Which type of tree has a broader crown spread?

HOWS & WHYS: Although a tree's species, age, and environment are the main factors that affect its height and crown spread, conifers often grow upward and deciduous trees branch out more to the sides. You are more likely to find a deciduous tree with a rounded shape, short height, and wide crown spread.

S T E A M Foresters like you use a combination of botany and geometry to calculate the size and shape of trees.

Now Try This!: Explore outdoors to find a group of similar trees that were planted at the same time. Measure their heights and think about why the trees might not all be the same height even if they are the same kind of tree and the same age. Are some of the trees in shade? This would slow their growth.

MEASURING MUD BRICKS

LEVEL OF DIFFICULTY:
MEDIUM

MESSY METER:
MEDIUM MESS

FROM BEGINNING TO END:
1 HOUR, PLUS
BRICK-DRYING TIME

SEASONS:

MATERIALS

- ¾ cup sand
- 1¼ cups soil
- 1⅓ cups water
- 1 set of measuring cups
- Bucket
- Garden trowel (a small shovel) or old spoon
- Ice cube tray

 Bricks are made by mixing clay with water, pouring the mixture into a mold, and drying the mixture until it is hard and strong. In this experiment, you will use different measurements of materials to find a recipe for making mud bricks. **Will more or less sand make a stronger brick?**

Hypothesis: ....

....

Caution: Always wash your hands and tools with soap and water after working with mud.

THE STEPS

1. On a sunny day, mix ½ cup of sand, ½ cup of soil, and ⅔ cup of water in a bucket.

2. Use a garden trowel or old spoon to press the mixture into the ice cube tray.

3. Let the mud bricks dry in the sun for 1 to 2 hours.

4. Turn the ice cube tray upside down to release the bricks.

5. Build a tower with the bricks. How many bricks can you stack before they crumble?

6. In the same bucket, mix ¼ cup of sand, ¾ cup of soil, and ⅔ cup of water.

7. Use a garden trowel or old spoon to press the mixture into ice cube tray.

8. Let the mud bricks dry in the sun for 1 to 2 hours.

9. Turn the ice cube tray upside down to release the bricks.

10. Build a tower with the bricks. How many bricks can you stack before they crumble?

HOWS & WHYS: Soil has three types of material: **clay** (which is sticky), **loam** (which is fluffy), and **sand** (which is crumbly). Clay is great for making bricks because it sticks together. Sand is not great for making bricks because it crumbles. The more clay and the less sand in a brick, the stronger it will be.

S T E A M Testing and comparing two different mud brick recipes involves **science and chemical engineering.**

Now Try This!: Try mixing clay into your bricks. Can you find an even better brick recipe?

SNOWFLAKES IN THE WILD

LEVEL OF DIFFICULTY:
MEDIUM
MESSY METER: MINOR MESS
FROM BEGINNING TO END:
1 HOUR
SEASON:

MATERIALS

- Snowstorm
- 1 piece of cold, black construction paper
- Magnifying glass or hand lens
- ¼ cup water
- Dropper (optional)

 People often say that no two snowflakes are alike. In this experiment, you will explore the shape of snowflakes by capturing snowflakes in the wild. You will learn how snowflakes form by making your own snowflakes. **What shape do snowflakes make, and how do snowflakes form?**

Hypothesis: ....

! **Caution:** Dress warmly when going outdoors in winter.

THE STEPS

1. Your paper needs to be cold to catch snowflakes without melting them. You can put your paper in a mailbox for 15 minutes to cool down without getting wet.

2. When snow is falling from the sky, set out a piece of black construction paper to catch 10 or more snowflakes.

3. Use a magnifying glass or hand lens to study the wild snowflakes that you caught.

4. What shapes do you see? Is there a shape that you see in more than one snowflake?

5. Bring ¼ cup of water outside and, using a dropper or your fingertips, drip tiny drops of water onto your construction paper to freeze into snowflakes.

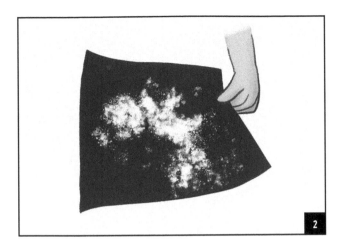

6. Let the water freeze for 15 to 30 minutes, then study your homemade snowflakes with a magnifying glass or hand lens.

7. What shapes do you see? Are the homemade snowflakes similar to or different than the snowflakes in the wild?

HOWS & WHYS: In the wild, snowflakes form very slowly. Over a long time in a cloud, water condenses from a gas to a solid, slowly building a **crystal**. The shape of water makes hexagonal, or 6-sided, crystals. Because snowflakes form very slowly while gently swirling through clouds, many branches can grow, making beautiful shapes. Home-made snowflakes freeze so quickly that they won't make such fancy crystals.

S T E A M Understanding shapes like 6-sided hexagons is important in art, engineering, and math.

Now Try This!: For a fun art and math challenge, make paper snowflakes. Begin with a piece of square paper. Fold the paper in half diagonally to make a triangle. Repeat to make a smaller triangle. Fold this triangle into thirds, then cut shapes out of the sides using scissors. Unfold the paper to see your snowflake!

GRAVITY DROP

LEVEL OF DIFFICULTY:
MEDIUM
MESSY METER: MINOR MESS
FROM BEGINNING TO END:
30 MINUTES
SEASONS:

MATERIALS

- 3 objects with different shapes and weights, such as stones, feathers, sticks, flowers, leaves, and seeds
- Stopwatch, such as the clock app on a smartphone

 Gravity pulls all objects down to Earth, but when different objects are dropped from the same height, they don't always fall at the same speed. **Why do some objects fall faster than others?**

Hypothesis: _____

_____

Caution: Always have an adult supervise when you climb to a height.

THE STEPS

1. Explore outdoors, searching for 3 objects with different shapes and weights. For example, a small rock, a feather, a stick, or an acorn, a flower, and a cattail.

2. Carry your 3 objects to a high outdoor place, such as the top of a set of stairs or a high rock. Be sure to have an adult supervise to help you stay safe.

3. Pick up all 3 objects and hold them all together in one hand.

4. Drop all 3 objects and watch them fall.

5. Pick up your 3 objects and carry them to the same high place.

6. Choose the object that landed first. Drop it again, but this time, use the stopwatch to measure how long it takes to fall. Start the stopwatch at the same time that you drop the object and stop the stopwatch when it lands.

7. Repeat step 6 to measure how long it takes for the object that landed second to fall. Was the time different?

8. Repeat step 6 to measure how long it takes for the object that landed last to fall. What do you notice?

HOWS & WHYS: When an object is falling through the air, another force comes into play: air! The air actually slows the object's fall. The more an object touches the air, the more the air slows its fall. A light object that takes up a lot of space will touch the air more than a heavy object, and it will fall more slowly than a heavy object that takes up a little space.

S T E A M Because you repeated your experiment 3 times, you used science in this math activity.

Now Try This!: To calculate the average time it takes an object to fall from a certain height, drop that object 3 times. Use the stopwatch to measure the time for each fall. Add the 3 times together and divide that number by 3.

OLD AS THE TREES

LEVEL OF DIFFICULTY: HARD

MESSY METER: MINOR MESS

FROM BEGINNING TO END:
45 MINUTES

SEASONS:

MATERIALS

- Tree (You must know the name of the type of tree, or tree species. For example, red maple or white oak.)
- Flexible tape measure, or a piece of string and a ruler
- Masking tape or marker
- Calculator

? You can discover the age of a tree after it's been cut down by counting the rings in its stump. Most of the time, foresters don't want to cut down trees. **How can you discover the age of a tree without cutting it down?**

Hypothesis: _____

_____

THE STEPS

1. Go to a tree. Use a tape measure to find a spot on the bark 4½ feet (54 inches) above the ground. Mark this spot with a piece of tape or marker.

2. Wrap the flexible tape measure around the tree trunk at the marked spot.

3. Be careful to keep the tape measure flat and horizontal. Don't let it slide down the tree trunk.

4. Where the 0-inch mark meets the tape measure, you will see the number showing the circumference, or distance around, the tree trunk.

5. Use a calculator to divide the tree's circumference by 3.14 (pi). The answer will be the **diameter** of the tree trunk, or the distance across the tree trunk at its widest point.

6. Foresters have studied the **diameter at breast height (DBH)**, or diameter of a tree 4½ feet from the ground, of many tree species. If you multiply the DBH of your tree by its **growth factor** in the table below, you will know your tree's age in years. Now that's some tree-rific math!

Tree species	Age of tree
Dogwood	7.0 x DBH
Douglas fir	5.0 x DBH
Loblobby pine	5.0 x DBH
Northern red oak	4.0 x DBH
Quaking aspen	2.0 x DBH
Red maple	4.5 x DBH
Sugar maple	5.5 x DBH
Sweetgum	4.0 x DBH
White oak	5.0 x DBH

CONTINUED

HOWS & WHYS: Every spring, trees grow new wood just under their bark. The new wood has a special texture that makes a new ring. Foresters can study tree stumps to look at these rings and discover how much each tree species grows in a year and calculate the growth factors. Because many trees, especially trees growing in cities and gardens, have a different habitat than forest trees, growth factor tables give an **estimate**, or rough guess, of a tree's age.

Ⓢ①ⒺⒶⓂ In addition to using the math functions of division and multiplication, you used measuring and calculation technologies in this experiment.

Now Try This!: To discover your tree's birthday, subtract its age from the current year. Research this year to learn about what events happened the year your tree first sprouted.

SPOTLIGHT ON: ASTRONOMERS!

Astronomers are scientists who study the universe, including all of the stars and galaxies that exist. Astronomers chart the paths of the planets in our solar system as they orbit around the sun, and measure the paths of meteors and comets as they streak through the sky. In addition to using math to count, track, and predict the movements of stars and planets, astronomers use many advanced technologies, including telescopes, instruments that make distant objects look nearer. Today's telescopes can take photographs so that astronomers don't have to stay up all night. If you love math and studying the night sky, you might want to explore career opportunities in astronomy. Most astronomy jobs involve teaching at colleges and universities.

Chapter Seven

PUTTING IT ALL TOGETHER

Through the experiments in this book, you have learned how to use science, technology, engineering, art, and math to explore and understand the outdoors. Look back at the many projects you have done, and think about what you learned. Do you know more about how the moon moves through space? Do you understand more about how pine cones keep seeds dry in a rainstorm? I hope that you have enjoyed your STEAM projects and had fun sharing what you learned with friends and family members.

No matter which experiments you chose to do, you have learned so much about the scientific method. Now more than ever, you can explore questions, make and test predictions, collect and analyze data, and draw conclusions about the world. These skills will come in handy every time you consider a new investigation or try to understand one of nature's many mysteries.

As a young scientist, you will be able to see and imagine more and more of what is really happening when a maple tree's seeds helicopter to the ground or a stone sinks into a river. When you walk through the world, remember to think about the science taking place outdoors. Notice what is happening around you. If you don't know how it works yet, you can get to the bottom of it by using your awesome STEAM skills. Every time you investigate the amazing outdoors, you contribute to the science of nature!

RESOURCES

BOOKS

Let's Go Rock Collecting by Roma Gans, illustrated by Holly Keller. Learn about how rocks are formed.

Messy Maths: A Playful, Outdoor Approach for Early Years by Juliet Robertson. Outdoor math activities for young children.

Owl Moon by Jane Yolen, illustrated by John Schoenherr. A father and child look for owls on a moonlight night.

Rhoda's Rock Hunt by Molly Beth Griffin, illustrated by Jennifer A. Bell. A young girl discovers the wonderful world of rocks.

The Berenstain Bears' Big Book of Science and Nature by Stan and Jan Berenstain. Have fun reading about the Bears' adventures in science.

Winter Tree Finder by May Theilgaard Watts and Tom Watts. Everything you need to know to discover trees in winter.

WEBSITES AND ORGANIZATIONS

American Chemical Society: Adventures in Chemistry. Chemistry lessons and activities for kids of all ages from America's top chemistry teachers. ACS.org/content/acs/en/education/whatischemistry/adventures-in-chemistry.html

Carolina Biological Supply. Purchase termites and other life science supplies. Carolina.com

Exploratorium. Science resources and activities to try at home. Exploratorium.edu

iNaturalist. Download an app on your phone for recording nature observations. Share what you find with professional naturalists and discuss your findings. iNaturalist.org

Journey North. Help scientists save monarch butterflies, hummingbirds, and more. JourneyNorth.org

Kids Love Rocks. Materials and activities for learning about rocks. KidsLoveRocks.com

Land Art for Kids. Step-by-step ideas for creating land art. LandArtForKids.com

Laughing Kids Learn. Homeschool blog with DIY learning activities. LaughingKidsLearn.com

Minnesota Department of Natural Resources: Teach Outdoors Program. Outdoor lessons for kids of all ages. DNR.State.MN.us/education/teachers/outdoor-lessons.html

National Geographic Kids. Games, videos, and more. Kids.NationalGeographic.com

National Kid Wind Challenge. Order a DIY wind turbine kit and design your own at home. KidWind.org

Project FeederWatch from The Cornell Lab of Ornithology. Help scientists track bird activity from your own backyard. FeederWatch.org

Ranger Rick. Crafts, activities, games, and videos from the National Wildlife Federation. RangerRick.org

Science Sparks. Science experiments for kids, organized by grade level. Science-Sparks.com

Sciencing. Homework help, projects, experiments, and news. Sciencing.com/about-us

Smithsonian Magazine. Great explanations for every mystery in the world. SmithsonianMag.com

Steve Spangler Science. Fun STEAM toys, science experiments, and hands-on activities. SteveSpanglerScience.com

The USA National Phenology Network. Track the seasons with professional scientists. USANPN.org/usa-national-phenology-network

GLOSSARY

ABSORB: Soak up

AGRONOMIST: A scientist who manages soil for the best food crops

AIR PRESSURE: Force pressing down on Earth from the weight of the air in the atmosphere

ANEMOMETER: Tool for measuring the speed of wind

ANGLE: The space between two lines, surfaces, or objects

ANTENNAE: Long, thin feelers that bugs and other animals use to sense their environment

ARCHITECTURE: The art and science of designing buildings

ASTRONOMER: A scientist who studies the sun, moon, planet, stars, and galaxies

BAROMETER: Tool measuring atmospheric pressure

BIOMIMICRY: Invention and design inspired by living things

BOTANIST: Plant scientist

BOTANY: Science of plants

CARDINAL DIRECTIONS: North, south, east, and west

CARTOGRAPHERS: Mapmakers

CELLULAR RESPIRATION: When cells use oxygen to break down food chemicals, making energy

CENTRIPETAL FORCE: A force that keeps an object moving in a curved path by pulling inward

CHLOROPHYLL: Green chemical that makes photosynthesis possible

CHOICE CHAMBERS: A tool that gives small creatures two or more mini environments to choose from

CLAY: Soil particles that are small and sticky

COMPASS: A tool used in navigation that uses a magnet to point to the direction north

COMPASS ROSE: A diagram showing the directions north, south, east, and west that is usually on a compass

COMPOST: Leaves, plant-based food scraps, and other materials that are broken down into a rich fertilizer

CONDENSATION: When a gas cools and changes to a liquid

CONIFEROUS: A tree or shrub with cones

CONTROL: A version of an experiment that matches the main experiment but doesn't have the factor that is being tested; a control gives baseline data and can be compared with the main experiment to measure the impact of the factor being tested

CROWN SPREAD: The distance that a tree's branches reach horizontally at their maximum width

CRUSTACEANS: Animals with hard exteriors, antennae, and gills

CRYSTAL: A solid material with a highly organized microscopic structure

CURRENT: Water or air moving in one direction

DATA: Scientific information, usually collected in an experiment

DECIDUOUS: A tree or shrub that drops its leaves in the fall

DENSITY: A measurement of how much matter is packed into a certain amount of space

DIAMETER: The distance across a circle

DIAMETER AT BREAST HEIGHT (DBH): The distance across the trunk of a tree 4½ feet from the ground

DISTILLED: Liquid that has been boiled and condensed

DYE: Chemical that adds color

EARTHWORKS: Art created by reshaping the land

ECLIPSE: When a body in a solar system is covered by a shadow

ENDANGERED: A species very much at risk of going extinct

ENGINEERING: Science and technology used to solve problems

ENGINEERING DESIGN: A cycle that involves finding a problem, creating and testing solutions, and retesting solutions so that they work even better

ENTOMOLOGY: Science of insects

ENVIRONMENT: The space or habitat that surrounds a living thing

ENVIRONMENTAL ENGINEERING: Engineering focused on solving environmental problems, including pollution

EROSION: When rain and wind push soil off the land and into rivers, removing valuable nutrients and polluting waterways with dirt.

ESTIMATE: An inexact or rough guess, usually for a number

EVAPORATION: When a liquid heats up and becomes a gas

FOLIATED: A rock with lined-up minerals that make sheetlike layers

FORESTER: A person who works as a forest manager

FLUTTER: A group of butterflies

FRICTION: The resistance to movement that happens when two objects rub together

GALAXY: Millions or billions of stars in a group held together by gravity

GEOLOGIST: A scientist who studies the Earth, including rocks.

GEOLOGY: Earth science

GRAVITY: The force that pulls objects down to Earth

GROWTH FACTOR: A number that, when multiplied by a tree's diameter at breast height, gives the tree's age in years

HERBARIUM: A scientific collection of dried plants

HIBERNATION: A seasonal sleeplike rest

HORTICULTURE: The art and science of gardening

HYDROLOGIST: A scientist who studies water

HYDROPONICS: Growing plants without soil, usually in nutrient-rich water

HYDROSCOPIC: A material that absorbs water vapor from the air

IDENTIFY: To discover what something is

IGLOO: An Inuit dome-shaped building made from blocks of snow

IGNEOUS: Rock formed from melted rock that cooled

INFRARED: A type of radiation given off by hot objects

INSULATION: Material that stops heat, electricity, or sound from escaping

KALEIDOSCOPE: A group of butterflies

LIFT: A force that goes against gravity to hold an airplane in the air

LOAM: Soil particles that are medium size and fluffy

LUNAR: About the moon

MECHANICAL ENGINEERING: Engineering focused on machines

METAMORPHIC: Rock that was changed by intense heat or pressure

METEOROLOGIST: Weather scientist

METEOROLOGY: The science of weather

MODEL: A representation of a process, idea, or object used to understand it

NUTRIENTS: A chemical that nourishes growth or life

OBSERVATION: What you notice about something

ORBIT: The path of an object in space as it moves around another object

PARALLEL: Side-by-side relationship between two lines, surfaces, or objects

PHASES (OF MATTER): The states that matter can have: solid, liquid, or gas

PHASES (OF THE MOON): The different ways the moon appears to us on Earth

PHENOLOGY: Science of the season cycles for living things

PHEROMONE: A chemical released by an animal that impacts another animal

PHOTOCHEMISTRY: Science of matter and light

PHOTOSENSITIVE: Responding to light

PHOTOSYNTHESIS: The process of turning sunlight energy, water, and carbon dioxide into sugar and oxygen

PHYSICS: The science of matter, energy, and the forces in the universe

PREDICT: To say what will happen in the future

RAIN GAUGE: A tool for collecting and measuring rain

REFRACTION: Bending of light when it goes from one material to another (like from air to water)

RHIZOID: Plant part that anchors and absorbs water

SAND: Soil particles that are large and crumbly

SATELLITE: A tool that orbits Earth to collect information

SCALE: Distance relationships; for example, 1 inch on a map representing 1 mile in the real world

SCALES (ON A PINE CONE): Small, thin, overlapping plates that protect the seeds within a pine cone

SEDIMENTARY: Rock that forms when materials settle and harden

SOLAR: About the sun

STILL: A tool that distills liquid through boiling and condensing it

STOMATA: Small openings in the surface of a leaf

SUNDIAL: A tool that tells the time by casting a shadow in the sun's light

SUSTAINABLE ENERGY: Power source that grows back and does not run out

SWARM: A group of insects, such as butterflies

TERRACE: A flat area carved into a hill

ULTRAVIOLET: Light waves that are shorter than violet light and very high energy

UPCYCLE: To reuse something in a way that makes it better

VALLEY: A low area between hills or mountains

VENATION: Pattern of veins in a leaf

VOLUME: A measurement of space

WATER CYCLE: How water moves from oceans to clouds to the land

WATERSHED: An area of land where all of the water flows to the same lake, river, or ocean

WAVELENGTH: The length of a wave, from a low point to the next low point

WIND TURBINE: A machine that captures wind energy and converts it to electricity

INDEX

ACKNOWLEDGMENTS

Many thanks to the amazing staff at Belwin Conservancy, Audubon Center of the North Woods, Wolf Ridge Environmental Learning Center, Outward Bound, National Park Service, Mississippi Park Connection, Friends of the Mississippi River, Youth Farm, Como Zoo and Conservatory, the Minnesota Zoo, Baker Park Reserve, and Gale Woods Farm, for a lifetime of incredible outdoor science adventures. I am so grateful to teach at Open World Learning Community, an EL Education school, where my colleagues are committed to going the extra mile to facilitate meaningful, memorable field work. Thanks to my principal for approving my field trip requests, and to my students for showing me how to appreciate and advocate for our environment. Every time I step out into the field, be it as a teacher, parent, or a tree hugger, the connection between learning and being outside is affirmed.

ABOUT THE AUTHOR

Dr. Megan Olivia Hall, PhD, NBCT is the 2013 Minnesota Teacher of the Year. As a science, robotics, and agriculture teacher, Megan has worked with learners of many ages and levels, from kindergarteners to graduate students. A National Board-certified teacher, she serves as science department chair and develops anti-racist social-emotional curricula at Open World Learning Community in St. Paul Public Schools. Megan's writing has been featured in *Education Week* and *The Science Teacher*. She is the author of the book *Awesome Kitchen Science Experiments for Kids*. A Leading Educator Ambassador for Equity Fellow with the Education Civil Rights Alliance, Megan holds a PhD in learning, instruction, and innovation from Walden University. She is a certified yoga instructor who loves to read, garden, and play outdoors.

Printed in the USA
CPSIA information can be obtained
at www.ICGtesting.com
CBHW050337310524
9306CB00011B/141